50 GREAT
Bed & Breakfasts
— AND INNS —

NEW ENGLAND

Susan Sulich

RUNNING PRESS
PHILADELPHIA · LONDON

Books published by Running Press are available at special discounts for bulk purchases in the United States by corporations, institutions, and other organizations. For more information, please contact the Special Markets Department at the Perseus Books Group, 2300 Chestnut Street, Suite 200, Philadelphia, PA 19103, or call (800) 810-4145, ext. 5000, or e-mail special.markets@perseusbooks.com.

ISBN 978-0-7624-5747-2

Library of Congress Control Number: 2015933488

E-book ISBN 978-0-7624-5801-1

9 8 7 6 5 4 3 2 1
Digit on the right indicates the number of this printing

EDITOR Linda Falken
DESIGNER Tim Palin Creative

Running Press Book Publishers
2300 Chestnut Street
Philadelphia, PA 19103-4371

Visit us on the web!
www.offthemenublog.com

CONTENTS

VERMONT

MAINE

INTRODUCTION

Hundreds of vacation experiences await the traveler in the six New England states. From skiing on powdery snow-covered mountains, to gathering shells on sandy beaches, to driving a scenic road when the fall foliage is setting the hills ablaze with spectacular color, the offerings multiply with the passing seasons.

Bed and breakfasts and inns, each with its own personality and style, offer unique accommodations from which to explore the region. The lodgings become part of the adventure, with unexpected surprises awaiting you at every turn: period furnishings, charming gardens, innkeepers, and guests with interesting stories to tell.

Breakfast, that most humble of meals (often filled with meager and unimaginative fare or skipped altogether), gets top billing when you stay at one of these establishments, and many of the recipes are inspired by the region. Indulge in Lobstah Eggs (page 241) as you sit at a table overlooking a Maine harbor and watch the boats bob in the waves while imagining the wonders that await you at spectacular Acadia National Park. Savor a slice of fresh-out-of-the-oven Cranberry-Zucchini Bread (page 133) as you ponder the path of the first pilgrims in Plymouth, Massachusetts. Enjoy a bowl of Maple Granola (page 208) during maple-sugaring season in the heart of Vermont. These are just a few of the mouthwatering ways to start your day that you'll find within these pages.

Before setting out to see art exhibits, wine trails, and living history museums, your palate can explore new breakfast flavors with imaginative combinations, like Duck and Green Chile Hash with Poached Eggs and Chipotle Hollandaise (page 168), Maple-Banana-Bacon Muffins (page 144), and Mascarpone Cheese and Fruit-Stuffed French Toast Croissants (page 24).

This book will take you on a tour of the most unique, luxurious, and welcoming bed and breakfasts and inns in New England. They are found snuggled into mountainsides, dotting the endless miles of shoreline, and standing guard on the main streets of quaint towns. Many are situated to take full advantage of New England's diverse and breathtaking landscapes, with features such as an outdoor hot tub, where you can feel the cares of the world ebb away as you listen to the waves washing up on a nearby beach, or a breakfast room with floor-to-ceiling windows that bring the outdoors right up to your orange juice. When was the last time there was something worth lingering over with your coffee?

New England also offers a doorway to the past and is richly steeped in early American history. Scouting antiques on Connecticut country roads, you can time-travel back to our country's early days and truly immerse yourself in the time period by lodging at a bed and breakfast that's furnished with colonial period pieces, then greet the morning with Applesauce Parfait (page 25) made with New England brown bread, a recipe the earliest settlers learned from the Native Americans, or maybe some Cranberry-Walnut Scones (page 114), a holdover from Mother England. The traveler who wants a more diverse weekend can stay over at an inn where Robert Todd Lincoln and President William Howard Taft may once have supped, and wake up to an Apple-Cheddar Quiche (page 184), made with Vermont's most famous cheddar, before heading out for a day of outlet shopping.

It's safe to say that there is an appealing New England getaway for everyone. The diversity of activities, accommodations, and menus affords limitless possibilities. You could visit all fifty inns in the book and have a distinctly different adventure at each one.

As you use this book, you'll find a few easily identifiable features to help inform you. Tasty Tidbits shares fun foodie facts; Sweet Additions gives you variations on recipes; Local Color reveals interesting trivia and historical bits; and Things to Do offers suggestions for both well- and little-known excursions within striking distance of the inns and B&Bs.

50 Great Bed & Breakfasts and Inns—New England tells you where to go, what you'll find when you get there, and how to bring a delicious slice of your trip back home. Get a cup of coffee and thumb through the pages. You'll be enticed by recipes you'll want to serve your family for breakfast or to guests for a festive brunch. You'll also be inspired to start planning your next New England getaway.

Godspeed and *bon appétit!*

—Susan Sulich

The Daniel Rust House

The Inn at Kent Falls

Hidden Valley Bed
and Breakfast

Fitch Claremont Vineyard
Bed and Breakfast

The Wallingford
Victorian Inn

The Copper
Beech Inn

Bee and
Thistle Inn

Steamboat
Inn

Scranton Seahorse Inn

Connecticut

When I was a child, I saw lots of movies about happy people living in Connecticut. And ever since then, that was where I wanted to live. I thought it would be like the movies. And it really is. It's exactly what I hoped it would be.

—Polly Bergen

BEE AND THISTLE INN

The Bee and Thistle Inn was built in 1756 as a residence for Judge William Noyes and his family. The house was originally set near the Boston Post Road but was moved back to its present position and restored by the Hodgson family at the turn of the last century. A sunken garden and inviting porches were added at that time.

100 Lyme Street
Old Lyme, CT 06371
860-434-1667
www.beeandthistleinn.com

"Legendary" Scones

In the Bee and Thistle's earlier days, scones with honey were a staple at dinner. Today, these renowned treats are served for both breakfast and afternoon tea at the inn.

Sweet Additions

While the scones are delicious just the way they are, you can vary the flavor by adding 4 tablespoons of diced or small plump dried fruits, such as currants, raisins, apricots, or figs, to the dough at the same time that you add the zest.

"Legendary" Scones

Yields 12 scones

3 cups all-purpose flour

⅓ cup granulated sugar, plus
    4 tablespoons for sprinkling
    on top

2½ teaspoons baking powder

½ teaspoon baking soda

¾ teaspoon salt

¾ cup (1½ sticks) cold unsalted
    butter, cut into small pieces

1 cup buttermilk, plus more as
    needed

1 tablespoon grated orange or
    lemon zest

¼ cup heavy cream

1. Position the oven racks to divide the oven into thirds and preheat to 400°F.

2. In a medium bowl, stir the flour, ⅓ cup of the sugar, baking powder, baking soda, and salt together with a fork. Add the cold butter pieces and, using your fingertips, a pastry blender, or two knives, work the butter into the dry ingredients until the mixture resembles coarse cornmeal. It's okay if some largish pieces of butter remain—they'll add to the flakiness of the scones.

3. Pour in the buttermilk, toss in the zest, and mix with the fork only until the ingredients are just moistened. You should have a soft dough with a rough look. (If the dough looks dry, add another tablespoon of buttermilk.)

4. Gather the dough into a ball, pressing it gently so that it holds together. Turn it out onto a lightly floured work surface and knead it very briefly; a dozen turns should do it.

5. Cut the dough in half.

6. Roll one piece of the dough into a ½-inch-thick circle about 7 inches across. Brush the dough with half of the heavy cream, sprinkle with 2 tablespoons of sugar, and cut the circle into 6 triangles. Place the scones on an ungreased baking sheet and repeat with the remaining half of the dough.

7. Bake the scones for 10 to 12 minutes, or until both the tops and bottoms are golden. Transfer the scones to a rack to cool slightly. The scones are best served warm but are just fine at room temperature.

Explore Local Arts

The town of Old Lyme was home to a famous art colony from 1899 to 1937. Its founder, landscape artist Henry Ward Ranger, said the area was reminiscent of pastoral scenes of the lowlands and coastal areas of Holland. The beautiful scenery attracted many artists who would take their easels outside to paint *en plein air*.

Childe Hassam, *Church at Old Lyme, Connecticut, 1905*

The Lyme Art Colony was key to the development of the American Impressionist movement, due in no small part to its most famous member, Childe Hassam. The hub of the colony was a boarding house owned by Florence Griswold, located right next door to the Bee and Thistle. Today, the Griswold home is a museum (860-434-5542 or visit www.flogris.org) showcasing the works of American Impressionists. There are several other galleries and art associations in the town, which continues to be a strong supporter of the arts.

The Fox and the Pineapple is by Brian Keith Stephens, a local artist whose work is shown at the Bee and Thistle.

The Bee and Thistle shares this love of art and honors the town's tradition by featuring the works of local artists in the inn and on its grounds. Sculptures dot its five and a half acres, and works in many mediums, including photography, pen and ink, oil, and textile screen printing, decorate the walls of the common areas and the rooms at the inn. Guests can learn about the art and the artists from the Bee and Thistle's gallery catalog and even arrange to purchase one of the artworks to take home.

THE WALLINGFORD VICTORIAN INN

This grand Queen Anne Victorian was built in 1890. The house was a wedding gift to Georgianna Simpson Hull and Charles Tibbits from her parents. Her father, Gurdon W. Hull founded Simpson, Hall & Miller Company, a prominent silver manufacturer that eventually became International Silver Company. The inn is an outstanding example of Victorian design. Its many exquisitely crafted hallmarks include hipped slate roofs capped with finials; textured, multipatterned shingles and clapboards; latticed porches; and intricate relief work.

245 North Main Street
Wallingford, CT 06492
203-265-1200
www.thewallingfordvictorian.com

Beet Pancakes with Ricotta Stars

Drizzle syrup or honey on these pancakes and serve
with sausage links and dry, scorched peach slices.

The New Englander

This tasty breakfast consists of eggs over easy with corned beef and
lentil hash accompanied by fresh-caught Atlantic salmon.

*The shores of Connecticut have always been an abundant source of
fresh seafood. Atlantic salmon, drizzled with a vinegar reduction,
gives this traditional breakfast a regional flair.*

Beet Pancakes with Ricotta Stars

Yields about 12 4-inch pancakes

1 cup tapioca pearls

2 cups all-purpose flour

2 large beets, peeled, shredded and placed in a sieve to drain (about 1½ cups)

½ teaspoon cinnamon

3 large eggs

12 ounces sparkling water

½ cup high-quality farm-fresh ricotta

1 teaspoon ground nutmeg

1. Put 2 cups of water and the tapioca pearls in a small saucepan and cook on low heat for ½ hour, or until done.

2. Put the flour in a large bowl.

3. Fold in the beets and cinnamon.

4. Beat the eggs and pour them into the beet mixture.

5. Slowly mix in enough sparkling water to create a thin batter (a little more than a cup should be enough).

6. Pour scoopfuls of batter onto a hot, greased griddle or skillet and cook until bubbly on one side, about 3 to 4 minutes. Flip the pancakes over and finish cooking.

7. Whip the ricotta cheese together with the nutmeg. Put the mixture in a pastry bag with a star tip and pipe stars on top of the pancakes.

■ ■ ■ ■ ■ ■ ■ ■ ■ ■ ■ ■

Tasty Tidbit

A famous sweet treat has its home in the state of Connecticut. In Orange, you'll find the PEZ factory and museum. First created in Austria in 1929, these small, pressed candies immigrated to the United States in the 1950s. To make the candy more popular in this country, the company began producing its signature dispensers in fun shapes and with cartoon characters, which are now collectors' items. You can visit the factory to learn more about the candy's history and to actually see PEZ in production. Go to www.pez.com for more information.

■ ■ ■ ■ ■ ■ ■ ■ ■ ■ ■ ■

The New Englander

Yields 4 servings

4 cups lentils

1 pound corned beef, uncooked and diced small

1⅓ cups chopped onion

4 cornichons, chopped fine

12 ounces fresh salmon

Salt and pepper

8 large eggs

4 handfuls arugula and baby kale

Vinegar Reduction (box, below), for drizzling

1. Steam or boil the lentils until cooked, about ½ hour.

2. Lightly coat a small sauté pan with olive oil and place on medium heat.

3. Add the corned beef to the pan and brown, stirring frequently.

4. Add the onion and continue cooking until the onion is soft and translucent.

5. Once the corned beef is browned and the onions are cooked, fold in the lentils.

6. Stir in the cornichons.

7. In a separate pan, season the salmon with salt and pepper and pan-sear up to 4 or 5 minutes per side, depending on desired doneness.

8. Cook the eggs over easy. Remove from the pan and throw in the arugula and baby kale to wilt slightly.

9. Put the greens on a plate and place the salmon on top. Drizzle the vinegar reduction over the salmon.

10. Add the eggs and hash.

Vinegar Reduction

You can easily make your own vinegar reduction. Start with 8 ounces of your favorite balsamic vinegar. Bring to a low boil and continue cooking until the vinegar is reduced down to about a third of what you started with and has a thick, syrupy consistency. Just be sure to open the windows when you do this because the steam from the cooking vinegar will sting your eyes and lungs!

THE COPPER BEECH INN

Named after the large copper beech tree growing in the front yard, this inn is situated in the quaint town of Ivoryton, which is dotted with colonial homes all along Main Street. Nearby are historic landmarks, including Gillette Castle, the highly acclaimed Ivoryton Playhouse and Goodspeed Opera House, antique and outlet shopping, and beach and shoreline attractions.

The Copper Beech Inn

46 Main Street
Ivoryton, CT 06442
860-767-0330
www.copperbeechinn.com

Buttermilk-Peach Pancakes

This is a guest favorite at the Copper Beech Inn. You can't go wrong with the classic combination of Bisquick and buttermilk for making perfect fluffy pancakes every time. However, if you wish, you can substitute your own favorite pancake mix. For maximum flavor, choose peaches from a local orchard and marinate them the evening before making the pancakes.

Stuffed Popovers

Popovers are never as good as when they first come out of the oven and should be served immediately after baking.

Tasty Tidbit

Popovers are an early American modification of the English Yorkshire pudding that New England settlers enjoyed back home.

Buttermilk-Peach Pancakes

Yields 4 servings

2 cups pancake mix (innkeeper's preference: Betty Crocker's Bisquick Original Pancake & Baking Mix)

2 tablespoons granulated sugar

2 teaspoons baking powder

½ teaspoon cinnamon

1½ cups buttermilk

1 large egg

Zest from ½ lemon

1½ cups diced fresh peaches, marinated in about 1 tablespoon peach preserves and a dash of peach brandy

Confectioners' sugar and mint leaves, for garnish

Sliced fresh peaches and Vermont maple syrup, for serving

1. In a medium bowl, mix the pancake mix, sugar, baking powder, and cinnamon.

2. Add the buttermilk, egg, and lemon zest, stirring with a fork or whisk until blended. Allow the batter to sit for a few minutes.

3. Place a griddle or skillet over medium-high heat. Grease with vegetable oil or, for added flavor, clarified butter. Pour the batter onto the hot griddle to the pancake size you prefer (about ¼ cup of batter will make a 4-inch pancake). Put some of the peaches on top. Cook until the edges of the pancake are dry and bubbles form on top, about 2½ minutes. Turn over and cook the other side until golden brown.

4. Sprinkle the pancakes with confectioners' sugar and garnish with mint leaves. Serve with sliced fresh peaches and Vermont maple syrup.

■ ■ ■ ■ ■ ■ ■ ■ ■ ■ ■ ■

Tasty Tidbit

If you're driving from the south via Interstate 95, you can stop along the way at one of Connecticut's foodie landmarks: Louis' Lunch (www.louislunch.com) in New Haven. Founded in 1895, Louis' Lunch claims to be the place where the hamburger sandwich was born. Legend has it that the hamburger was created when Louis slapped ground steak between two slices of toast in response to a customer's request for a fast lunch to go. Today, burgers are still cooked in the restaurant's antique vertical cast-iron gas grills and offered with cheese, tomato, or onion—but don't ask for ketchup or mustard; they are not allowed at Louis' Lunch.

■ ■ ■ ■ ■ ■ ■ ■ ■ ■ ■ ■

Stuffed Popovers

Yields 6 popovers

Batter:

1 tablespoon unsalted butter, melted and cooled

1 cup all-purpose flour

1½ teaspoons kosher salt

2 large farm-fresh eggs, at room temperature

1 cup whole milk, at room temperature

Filling:

1 teaspoon olive oil

3 farm-fresh eggs, beaten

½ cup diced heirloom tomatoes

¼ cup chopped scallions

1 tablespoon cream cheese

Salt and pepper

1. Preheat the oven to 400°F.

2. Grease a 6-cup popover pan with butter.

3. Combine the melted butter with the flour, salt, eggs, and milk in a food processor or blender and process for 30 seconds.

4. Divide the batter evenly among the cups of the popover pan, filling each cup one-third to one-half full. Bake on the middle rack of the oven for 40 minutes, taking care not to open the oven door. Remove the popovers to a cooling rack and pierce each one in the top with a knife to allow steam to escape.

5. Heat the olive oil in a sauté pan and add the eggs, tomatoes, and scallions.

6. Fold in the cream cheese. Use a rubber spatula to continuously fold the egg mixture until you reach a fluffy or desired consistency. Season with salt and pepper to taste.

7. Slice the popovers in half horizontally and spoon the egg filling into the bottom half. Put the top half back on and serve immediately.

THE DANIEL RUST HOUSE

Built in 1731 and originally called Bird in Hand, the B&B became a licensed tavern in 1800. The Daniel Rust House is decorated with period furnishings from the Colonial era. Each bedroom is named after one of the women who lived in the house. Outside, guests can enjoy a stroll around the two-acre grounds, replete with perennial gardens and fruit trees. University of Connecticut Storrs campus and Sturbridge Village are close by.

2011 Main Street
Coventry, CT 06238
860-742-0032
www.thedanielrusthouse.com

Mascarpone Cheese and Fruit-Stuffed French Toast Croissants

When the occasion calls for something special, consider this decadent French toast with its rich mascarpone filling and hint of Grand Marnier.

Applesauce Parfait

This recipe uses brown bread, a New England specialty.

Sweet Additions

The inn's stuffed French toast is a recipe for all seasons. It works just fine with fresh, frozen, or canned fruit, so you can take advantage of fresh strawberries, raspberries, blueberries, peaches, and other fruits when in season, and freeze or can any extra fruit— or use purchased frozen or canned fruit—to use in the off-season.

Mascarpone Cheese and Fruit-Stuffed French Toast Croissants

Yields 4 to 8 servings, depending on croissant size

2 cups half-and-half

6 large eggs

1 tablespoon vanilla extract

1 tablespoon Grand Marnier (optional)

8 croissants (innkeeper's preference: petite croissants)

8 ounces mascarpone cheese

1 cup fresh, frozen, or canned fruit (peach, blueberry, strawberry, or other)

12 ounces jam or preserves, same flavor as the fruit

2 tablespoons salted butter

Confectioners' sugar, for garnish

Maple syrup, for serving

1. Whisk together the half-and-half, eggs, vanilla, and Grand Marnier, if using.

2. Slice each croissant in half lengthwise.

3. Spread the cheese on the bottom half of each croissant, then layer on the fruit and the jam.

4. Put the top back on each croissant and then dip the filled croissant in the egg mixture for a few seconds.

5. Spread the butter on a heated griddle and cook the croissants until they are lightly browned on both sides and the cheese is melted, about 2 to 3 minutes per side.

6. Sprinkle with confectioners' sugar and serve with warm maple syrup.

Applesauce Parfait

Yields 6 to 8 servings, depending on glass size

¾ cup (1½ sticks) salted butter

1 can (16 ounces) brown bread
(innkeeper's preference: B&M)

1 jar (12 ounces) red currant jelly

1 jar (23 ounces) good-quality,
plain applesauce (not chunky)

2 to 3 tablespoons heavy cream

1. Melt the butter in a skillet over medium heat. Add the brown bread and, while it heats in the pan, chop the bread into small pieces with a spatula and mix well with the butter. Cook until the bread is moist, about 5 minutes. Do not overcook or the bread will become crumbly.

2. While the bread is cooking, put the red currant jelly in a small saucepan over low heat and cook until it is reduced to a syrupy consistency, about 1 to 2 minutes.

3. Once the bread has absorbed the butter and is nicely warmed through, take a parfait or other glass and put 1 tablespoonful of bread in the bottom. Add 1 tablespoon of applesauce and another layer of bread, then another tablespoon of applesauce. Top with a final spoonful of bread.

4. Add 1 heaping teaspoon of the jelly syrup (or a bit more to taste) on top of the layered bread and applesauce.

5. Top with a drizzle of heavy cream, to taste (but be careful not to drown the parfait in cream).

Tasty Tidbit

Brown bread dates back to the time of the Pilgrims. Native Americans taught early settlers how to steam-bake bread, and even today, many recipes for brown bread call for baking it in cans set in trays of water. The flour used is typically a mixture of whole wheat, rye, and cornmeal or jonnycake cornmeal.

FITCH CLAREMONT VINEYARD BED AND BREAKFAST

A working vineyard and thirty acres of farmland are the setting for this bed and breakfast. Originally built in 1790, the inn has been a farm, a public house, and finally the country estate of prominent industrialist Asa Fitch, whose renovations included a ballroom on the third floor and an outdoor racetrack, the remnants of which are still visible. Although it feels like it's in the middle of nowhere, the inn is only minutes from Foxwoods and Mohegan Sun Casinos. Best of all, wine from the vineyard is served with breakfast!

83 Fitchville Road
Bozrah, CT 06334
877-889-0266
www.fitchclaremonthouse.com

Apple Babies with Raspberry Swirl

The basic recipe is like a canvas you can paint various flavors on. Instead of apples, you can use any favorite or seasonal fruit.

Cantaloupe and Strawberries with Romanoff Sauce

You can vary this recipe with other melons and fruits in season. Honeydew melons with raspberries are a nice combination. If the strawberries are out of season or not quite sweet enough, feel free to add a little strawberry syrup as well as sugar.

Chocolate-Cinnamon Bread

Freshly made Chocolate-Cinnamon Bread is a delicious sweet breakfast treat.

Chocolate-Cinnamon French Toast with Raspberry Compote

Use day-old Chocolate-Cinnamon Bread to make the French toast— assuming there is enough left. You may have to make an extra loaf for the French toast.

Apple Babies
with Raspberry Swirl

Yields 4 servings

2 tablespoons salted butter, divided

4 large or 5 small eggs

¼ cup plus 1 tablespoon whole milk

Scant ¼ cup all-purpose flour
  (not self-rising)

Grating of fresh nutmeg or
  ⅛ teaspoon ground

1 Granny Smith apple, peeled, cored,
  and sliced into thin crescents

6 to 10 fresh raspberries

1 tablespoon dark brown sugar

½ teaspoon cinnamon

Confectioners' sugar, for garnish

1. Preheat the oven to 500°F (or as high as your oven will go).

2. Melt 1 tablespoon of the butter and mix it with the eggs, milk, flour, and nutmeg in an 8-ounce glass measuring cup or bowl.

3. Lightly coat 4 ramekins with vegetable cooking spray. Divide the egg mixture evenly between the 4 ramekins.

4. Melt the remaining 1 tablespoon of butter in a small skillet and add the apple slices and raspberries. Dot the fruit with brown sugar and cinnamon and lightly sauté until the apples are caramelized and al dente.

5. Arrange the cooked apple slices like the petals of a flower in each ramekin. Use a bit of the raspberry from the sauté for the flower center. Drizzle the remaining mixture around your apple flower.

6. Bake for 10 minutes, or until puffed and golden. Immediately slip each apple baby out of its ramekin and onto a plate. Sprinkle with confectioners' sugar and serve.

Cantaloupe and Strawberries with Romanoff Sauce

Yields 10 servings

Note advance prep time.

Sauce:

2 tablespoons confectioners' sugar

2 tablespoons light brown sugar

1 tablespoon rum extract

½ teaspoon orange zest

¼ teaspoon cinnamon

Grating of fresh nutmeg or
⅛ teaspoon ground

Fruit:

1 ripe cantaloupe, sliced into 10 wedges

5 or 6 strawberries, cut into very small
pieces and sugared to taste

1. Mix together all the ingredients for the sauce. Cover and refrigerate for 24 hours.

2. Undercut the melon wedges with a grapefruit knife and then cut into individual segments but leave them on the rind.

3. Spoon the sugared strawberries onto the melon wedges.

4. Drizzle a little sauce on top.

■ ■ ■ ■ ■ ■ ■ ■ ■ ■ ■ ■ ■

Tasty Tidbit

Connecticut is commonly referred to as "the Nutmeg State," even though that's not the state's official nickname. Several theories exist as to how this nickname came about. The most logical is that Connecticut sailors brought nutmeg back from where it was grown in the East Indies. This foray into the spice trade proved to be quite profitable for the sailors, and the nutmeg was much enjoyed by the colonists, who began using it in both sweet and savory dishes.

■ ■ ■ ■ ■ ■ ■ ■ ■ ■ ■ ■ ■

Chocolate-Cinnamon Bread

Yields 1 loaf

Note advance prep time.

1 package (16 ounces) pizza dough

2 heaping tablespoons Nutella

½ cup dark brown sugar, lightly packed and
 mixed with ½ teaspoon cinnamon

2 gratings fresh nutmeg or
 ¼ teaspoon ground

1 egg, beaten, mixed with a little water

½ cup confectioners' sugar

¼ teaspoon coconut extract

1. Coat a 9-inch springform pan with vegetable cooking spray.

2. Stretch out the dough with your hands and shape it into a 9- to 10-inch round. (Do not use a rolling pin.)

3. Spread the Nutella over the dough, leaving an inch between the Nutella and the edges of the dough. Sprinkle the Nutella with the sugar/cinnamon mixture and grate on the nutmeg.

4. Roll up the dough jelly-roll style and shape it into a round.

5. Place the dough in the springform pan, cover, and let it rise overnight in a warm place.

6. In the morning, preheat the oven to 400°F.

7. Brush the bread with the egg wash and bake it for 20 minutes, or until the bread is golden brown and sounds hollow when you tap on the top.

8. While the bread is baking, mix the confectioners' sugar, coconut extract, and 1½ teaspoons of water to make a glaze.

9. When the bread comes out of the oven, turn out of the pan immediately. Cool for ½ hour and then brush on the glaze.

Chocolate-Cinnamon French Toast with Raspberry Compote

Yields 4 servings

4 large eggs

2 tablespoons heavy whipping cream

1 teaspoon vanilla extract

½ teaspoon orange zest

1 tablespoon sifted, self-rising flour

4 slices day-old Chocolate-Cinnamon Bread (page 30)

Canola oil, for frying

1 recipe Raspberry Compote (below) and confectioners' sugar, for garnish

1. Whisk together the eggs, whipping cream, vanilla, orange zest, and flour in a medium bowl.

2. Dip the bread slices in the batter.

3. Pour canola oil into a skillet to the level of about ½ inch and place over medium heat.

4. Fry the bread slices until golden brown, about 2 minutes per side.

5. To serve, place a dollop of raspberry compote on top of each slice of French toast and sprinkle with confectioners' sugar.

Raspberry Compote

Note advance prep time.

1 cup fresh raspberries

¼ cup granulated sugar

1. Microwave the raspberries and sugar on high for 30 to 40 seconds. Do not let the mixture boil.

2. Refrigerate overnight before using.

HIDDEN VALLEY
BED AND BREAKFAST

An old-world-style manor, Hidden Valley Bed and Breakfast overlooks the nature preserve for which it is named. Guests can take in the magnificent view from the flagstone terrace with its inviting seating or enjoy a swim in the heated plunge pool. European furnishings give the inn an atmosphere of comfortable elegance.

226 Bee Brook Road
Washington Depot, CT 06794
860-868-9401
www.hiddenvalleyct.com

House Specialty

Baked Eggs

This dish, elegant in its simplicity and presentation,
is pleasing to both hosts and guests.

Local Color

While visiting Hidden Valley, consider a tour and
tasting at Hopkins Vineyard (www.hopkinsvineyard.com)
in nearby New Preston.

Baked Eggs

Yields 4 servings

4 tablespoons unsalted butter

4 large farm-fresh eggs

4 teaspoons finely chopped chives

Salt and coarsely ground pepper

4 toasted bread slices or croissants,
    for serving

1. Preheat the oven to 350°F.

2. Put 1 tablespoon of butter into each of 4 small ramekins and place in the oven to melt the butter.

3. When the butter has melted, break 1 egg into each ramekin and sprinkle each with 1 teaspoon of chives.

4. Bake the eggs until the yolk has reached the desired firmness, about 7 minutes for an egg with a cooked white and runny yolk

5. Sprinkle with salt and pepper.

6. Serve in ramekins with toasted bread or croissants.

■ ■ ■ ■ ■ ■ ■ ■ ■ ■ ■ ■

Tasty Tidbit

Baked eggs are also known as shirred eggs. First popular in the 1800s, shirred eggs experienced a resurgence in the 1950s and 1960s. They were traditionally cooked in a flat-bottomed dish called an egg shirrer, hence the name.

■ ■ ■ ■ ■ ■ ■ ■ ■ ■ ■ ■

Take a Hike

The Hidden Valley B&B looks out over the beautiful Hidden Valley Nature Preserve, which offers more than ten miles of hiking trails. Of particular note is the 820-foot-high Pinnacle, which offers a 270-degree view of the valley. At the Quartz Mine, the mineral formed as a massive white vein that was mined from the 1800s until 1915. Transported to the Hudson River by horse and wagon and, later, by train, the quartz was used as an abrasive and a paint filler.

At the nearby Steep Rock Preserve, a sloping dome of rock called the Clamshell is bordered on three sides by one of two side-by-side oxbows formed by the Shepaug River. Trails follow the curves of the river and loop around the sides of the Clamshell formation. Another trail takes you through a 235-foot-long tunnel built by the Shepaug Railroad in 1871–72 and used until the railroad closed down in 1948.

Biking and horseback riding are allowed on certain trails in both the Hidden Valley and Steep Rock Preserves. For details and maps, visit www.steeprockassoc.org, the website of the Steep Rock Association, which administers the preserves.

Not far to the northeast of the inn is the White Memorial Conservation Center (www.whitememorialcc.org), which features a nature museum and a wildlife sanctuary. Hikers can explore trails that run through much of the 4,000-acre preserve that encompasses fields, wetlands, and woodlands.

State Parks

Litchfield County is home to many state parks, which offer lots of opportunities for enjoying the area's natural beauty. Go to the state's Department of Energy and Environmental Protection (www.ct.gov/deep/site/default.asp) and click on the Parks & Forests heading to find information on individual parks. Some popular parks close to Hidden Valley B&B include:

Mount Tom

Black Rock

Lake Waramaug

Housatonic Meadows

SCRANTON SEAHORSE INN

Set in a quaint village close to the shore, this inn is housed in an 1833 Greek Revival-style home that was originally owned by Sereno Scranton. A prosperous and well-known citizen of Madison, Scranton owned many merchant ships and was the president of the Shoreline Railroad. He also served as a state representative and senator. Today, the Scranton Seahorse Inn features modern, luxurious accommodations within its historic walls.

818 Boston Post Road
Madison, CT 06443
203-245-0550
www.scrantonseahorseinn.com

Butternut Squash and Zucchini Crêpes with Sage Brown Butter

This is a great late summer recipe when zucchini is still thriving in the garden, and the butternut squash is just starting to come in. Make the crêpe batter the day before, then cook all the crêpes at once and stack them with parchment paper between each crêpe.

Kale Smoothie

Chock-full of good-for-you greens, this smoothie gets a hint of sweetness from the grapes.

Sweet Corn Flapjacks with Basil Butter

The innkeeper only makes this seasonal recipe when the summer corn and basil crops are going strong.

Apple Cider Bread with Currants

Cider and apples, two New England fall favorites, go into this unique quick bread.

Butternut Squash and Zucchini Crêpes with Sage Brown Butter

Yields 8 crêpes (4 servings)

Note advance prep time.

Batter:

1½ cups whole milk

4 large eggs

1½ cups all-purpose flour

1 pinch salt

½ cup (1 stick) unsalted butter, melted

Filling:

1 medium butternut squash, halved lengthwise and seeds removed

1 tablespoon extra-virgin olive oil

1 medium zucchini, diced

1 yellow onion, peeled and sliced thin

1 egg yolk

15 ounces whole-milk ricotta

1 cup cottage cheese

4 ounces cream cheese, at room temperature

½ teaspoon kosher salt

Pepper

2 to 3 tablespoons unsalted butter

Sage brown butter:

½ cup (1 stick) unsalted butter

3 to 4 fresh sage leaves

1. To make the batter, mix the milk, eggs, flour, and salt in a blender on medium speed until thoroughly combined.

2. With the blender on low speed, pour the melted butter through the opening on the lid, taking about 15 to 20 seconds. Let the batter sit in the refrigerator overnight in the blender or a covered bowl.

3. In the morning, take the batter out about an hour before you are ready to make the crêpes to allow it come to room temperature. Coat a nonstick crêpe pan or skillet with cooking spray and heat the pan over medium to high heat.

4. Add a small amount of batter to the pan and swirl it to evenly and thinly coat the pan. Once the edges turn brown, flip the crêpe and cook for 20 to 30 seconds more. Coat the pan with spray as needed and repeat with the remaining batter. Stack the crêpes with parchment paper between each one and set aside.

5. Preheat the oven to 300°F.

6. To make the filling, roast the butternut squash in a baking dish until soft, about 30 minutes. Remove from the oven and allow to cool.

7. While the squash cools, heat the olive oil in a nonstick pan over medium heat. Sauté the zucchini and onion until browned and soft, about 10 minutes. Remove from the pan and set aside. Once the squash has cooled, peel off the skin.

8. In a food processor, combine the butternut squash, egg yolk, ricotta, cottage cheese, and cream cheese and mix until very smooth. Add the salt and season with pepper to taste.

9. Place 2 tablespoons of the squash and cheese filling in the center of each crêpe and top with 1 tablespoon of the zucchini and onion mixture.

10. Fold in the sides of the crêpe to form a square and place each, seam-side down, on a sheet pan lined with parchment paper.

11. Melt 2 or 3 tablespoons of butter in a nonstick pan and brown the crêpes, adding more butter as needed. Return the browned crêpes to the sheet pan.

12. Heat the crêpes in the oven (still set at 300°F) for about 15 minutes.

13. While the crêpes are heating, make the sage brown butter. Melt 1 stick of butter over medium heat.

14. Add the sage leaves and heat until the butter is brown and aromatic, about 7 to 10 minutes, being careful not to burn it. Remove the sage leaves from the butter, chop and set aside.

15. When the crêpes are done heating, put one on each plate and drizzle with a generous teaspoon of the sage brown butter. Garnish with the chopped sage leaves.

Kale Smoothie

Yields 1 serving

2 cups red seedless grapes

½ cup cold filtered water, plus more as needed

4 to 5 stalks raw kale, rinsed and center stems removed

2 cups raw spinach

1 stalk celery, chopped coarse

1 banana (optional)

1. Put the grapes and water in a blender and purée until liquefied.

2. Add the kale, spinach, celery, and banana, if desired, and purée until smooth, adding more water or ice if needed.

Sweet Corn Flapjacks with Basil Butter

Yields 10 flapjacks

Basil butter:

1 cup (2 sticks) unsalted butter, softened to room temperature

1 teaspoon salt

Handful of basil leaves, stems removed and chopped

Pancakes:

2 tablespoons unsalted butter

2 ears of corn, cooked and kernels cut from cob

1 large egg

1¼ cups buttermilk

½ teaspoon baking soda

1¼ cups all-purpose flour

1 teaspoon baking powder

½ teaspoon kosher salt

2 teaspoons granulated sugar

2 tablespoons canola oil

Garnish:

Slices of fresh apples

1. Stir the 2 sticks of butter, salt, and basil leaves together.

2. Spoon the basil butter onto plastic wrap, roll it into a log, and refrigerate for at least an hour or overnight. (Unused butter can be stored in the refrigerator for up to 2 weeks.)

3. To start the pancakes, melt the 2 tablespoons of butter in a small saucepan over medium heat. Add the corn and toss to coat in the butter. Remove from the heat and set aside.

4. Whisk the egg, buttermilk, and baking soda thoroughly. Let stand for 5 minutes.

5. Sift the flour, baking powder, salt, and sugar into the buttermilk mixture and whisk until smooth.

6. Whisk in the canola oil and then fold in the buttered corn kernels.

7. Pour ⅓ cup of batter for each flapjack onto a hot, greased griddle and cook about 2 to 3 minutes, or until golden brown (lift an edge to look under and check). Then flip and cook for 2 more minutes.

8. To serve, top each flapjack with a slice of basil butter and some apple slices.

Apple Cider Bread with Currants

Yields 1 loaf

1 cup granulated sugar

1 cup light brown sugar, packed

¾ cup canola oil

3 large eggs, lightly beaten

2¼ cups all-purpose flour

1½ teaspoons baking soda

1 teaspoon kosher salt

1½ teaspoons cinnamon

¾ cup sour cream

1 cup fresh apple cider

1 teaspoon pure vanilla extract

2 of your favorite local crisp apples, peeled, cored, and grated (innkeeper's preference: Macoun or Granny Smith)

¾ cup currants

1. Preheat the oven 350°F.

2. Coat a 9 x 5-inch loaf pan with vegetable cooking spray and line with parchment paper.

3. In a medium bowl, whisk the sugars and oil until combined. Whisk in the eggs.

4. In another bowl, sift the flour, baking soda, salt, and cinnamon together.

5. In a third bowl, whisk together the sour cream, cider, and vanilla.

6. Add the flour mixture and the cider mixture to the egg mixture by thirds, using a large rubber spatula to fold in until just combined after each addition. Be careful to not overmix.

7. Fold in the grated apples and currants.

8. Pour the batter into the prepared loaf pan and bake on the center rack of the oven for 50 to 60 minutes, or until a tester inserted into the center of the loaf comes out clean. Let the loaf cool in the pan on a wire rack for 30 minutes before removing to cool completely.

THE INN AT KENT FALLS

Built in what was the original center of Kent in 1741, this inn, first called Flanders Arms, is listed in the National Register of Historic Places. Surrounded by natural beauty, guests can enjoy a hike at scenic Kent Falls State Park or a stroll through the quaint town. The inn is also within striking distance of the Berkshires. A stay at the Inn at Kent Falls, with its comfortable French antique style, colonial fireplaces, and screened porch, is like visiting a luxurious country estate.

107 Kent Cornwall Road
Kent, CT 06757
860-927-3197
www.theinnatkentfalls.com

Strawberry-Cinnamon Tea Bread

Enjoy this tea bread in the summer, when strawberries
are in season and at their sweetest.

Apple-Spice Tea Bread

Local apples abound in the fall, and this recipe is very appealing on a cool
day, accompanied by a cup of tea or coffee.

Lemon-Poppy Seed Tea Bread

This bread is very simple to make, but it doesn't sacrifice flavor for ease of
preparation. You can double the recipe and bake a batch of muffins, too.
Bake the muffins in muffin tins for 20 minutes.

Strawberry-Cinnamon Tea Bread

Yields 1 loaf

½ cup (1 stick) unsalted butter, softened

1½ cups granulated sugar, plus more for sprinkling on top

¼ teaspoon salt

2 large eggs

2 cups all-purpose flour

2 teaspoons baking powder

½ teaspoon cinnamon

½ cup whole milk or buttermilk

2 cups strawberries, cut into small pieces

1. Preheat the oven to 375°F. Grease and flour one 8½ x 4½-inch loaf pan.

2. Cream the butter with the sugar and salt until light and fluffy.

3. Beat in one egg at a time.

4. In a separate bowl, mix together the flour, baking powder, and cinnamon.

5. Lightly stir some of the dry ingredients into the batter, alternating with the milk, until both are totally incorporated into the batter.

6. Fold in the strawberries.

7. Scoop the batter into the prepared pan and sprinkle a little sugar on top.

8. Bake for 45 to 60 minutes, or until deep brown.

9. Cool the bread completely in the pan, or, if you can't wait, cool the bread briefly and lift it carefully from the pan.

Things to Do

Climb the Falls

A short but steep quarter-mile hike takes you to the top of Kent Falls, where it plunges 70 feet before cascading in a series of smaller falls to the valley and the Housatonic River. The Kent Falls State Park is part of the Viewpoints project, a joint effort of the Connecticut Commission on the Arts, the Connecticut Art Trail, and the Department of Energy and Environmental Protection. Outdoor exhibits reproduce paintings from the nineteenth century, showing how the state's landscape appeared more than a century ago. Visit www.arttrail.org for more information.

Apple-Spice Tea Bread

Yields 1 loaf

2 cups all-purpose flour

1 teaspoon cinnamon

1 teaspoon nutmeg

½ teaspoon allspice

1 teaspoon baking soda

½ teaspoon salt

1 cup (2 sticks) unsalted butter

2 cups granulated sugar

4 large eggs

1½ teaspoons vanilla extract

4 apples, peeled and chopped small

½ cup raisins or ¼ cup raisins and
   ¼ cup dried cranberries, rinsed in
   very warm water

1. Preheat the oven to 350°F. Grease and flour one 8½ x 4½-inch loaf pan.

2. In a medium bowl, mix together the flour, cinnamon, nutmeg, allspice, baking soda, and salt.

3. In a large bowl, cream together the butter, sugar, eggs, and vanilla until smooth.

4. Add the flour mixture to the butter mixture and mix.

5. Add the apples and raisins to the batter and mix until well combined.

6. Bake 55 to 60 minutes, or until a knife inserted in the center comes out clean.

7. Let the bread cool in the pan for a few minutes and then turn it out onto a cooling rack.

Lemon-Poppy Seed Tea Bread

Yields 1 loaf

3 cups all-purpose flour

1 cup granulated sugar

1½ teaspoons baking powder

1 teaspoon salt

1 cup (2 sticks) unsalted butter,
   very soft

3 large eggs

2 tablespoons poppy seeds

4 tablespoons freshly squeezed
   lemon juice

Zest from 2 lemons

1. Preheat the oven to 350°F. Grease and flour one 8½ x 4½-inch loaf pan.

2. Put all the ingredients in a large bowl and beat for 2 to 3 minutes, or until the batter is slightly fluffy.

3. Fill the prepared loaf pan three-quarters of the way with the batter.

4. Bake for 45 minutes, or until the bread is light in color and a knife inserted in the middle comes out clean.

5. Let the bread cool in the pan for a few minutes and then turn it out onto a cooling rack.

STEAMBOAT INN

Located in the heart of quaint, downtown Mystic, the Steamboat Inn has the distinction of offering the only waterfront accommodations in town. Nearly every room has beautiful views of the Mystic River, yet guests can step out the door and right into the historic district with its lovely shops and restaurants. Mystic Village, Mystic Aquarium, and the Mohegan Sun and Foxwoods Resort casinos are also close by.

73 Steamboat Wharf
Mystic, CT 06355
860-536-8300
www.steamboatinnmystic.com

Diana's Delectable Muffins

Born in the United Kingdom, the late Diana C. Stadtmiller was the innkeeper at Steamboat Inn for fifteen years. Her home traditions and warm sensibility helped shape the high standards and overall welcoming feeling of the inn. This much-requested recipe of hers is an all-time guest favorite.

Tasty Tidbit

Of all the fruits, only three—the blueberry, the Concord grape, and the cranberry—can trace their roots to North American soil.

Diana's Delectable Muffins

Yields about 18 muffins

4½ cups all-purpose flour

2 cups granulated sugar

4 teaspoons baking powder

1 teaspoon salt

4 large eggs

3 teaspoons vanilla extract

1 cup plain yogurt or 1 cup half-and-half

1 cup (2 sticks) salted butter, melted

1 cup whole milk

1 bag (12 ounces) frozen blueberries, raspberries, or cranberries, unthawed

(If fruit is tart, you can mix it with an additional ¼ to ½ cup of sugar before adding to the batter.)

1. Preheat the oven to 350°F.

2. Mix the flour, sugar, baking powder, and salt together in a bowl and set aside.

3. Mix the eggs, vanilla, yogurt, butter, and milk in a large bowl.

4. Add the dry ingredients to the wet ingredients and mix until combined.

5. Fold the fruit into the batter.

6. Fill each cup in the muffin tins to the top with batter.

7. Bake for 24 to 34 minutes, or until the tops of the muffins are golden.

Go to an Oyster Festival

Look for the Mystic Oyster Festival in August. The event features signature oyster dishes from a dozen restaurants, pairings with wine and beer, music, and activities for children. Proceeds benefit New England Science & Sailing, a community foundation that offers educational programs for families as well as for children and adults.

Oysters were consumed in great quantities by Connecticut's Native American inhabitants, who introduced them to the early European settlers. The shellfish soon became a staple in the colonists' diet. In fact, they were harvested in such quantities that laws regulating the taking of oysters were enacted in the early 1700s.

By the late nineteenth century, oyster farming was a major industry in Connecticut. During the 1890s, the state actually had the largest fleet of oyster steamers in the world. Today, Connecticut's oyster industry is still going strong. Thousands of bushels of oysters are sold throughout the country every year.

Given all that history, it's no wonder that oyster festivals are popular along the state's shoreline. Oyster festivals are also held in Norwalk and Milford, Connecticut, as well as in Wellfleet and Duxbury, Massachusetts.

State Shellfish

The eastern oyster (*Crassostrea virginica*) was declared Connecticut's state shellfish in 1989. This bivalve mollusk, which grows in the state's tidal rivers and coastal bays, is the most popular shellfish along the Connecticut shoreline. Prized for its exceptional quality, the eastern oyster is known for both its historic and current contributions to the state's economy.

The Pillsbury
House

Edgewood
Manor

William's
Grant Inn

Victorian
Ladies Inn

The Tower
House

Cliffside Inn

Ocean House

The 1661 Inn

Rhode Island

Rhode Island: It's like the period
at the end of a 49-word sentence.

—Anonymous

THE 1661 INN

1661 is the year that the first European settlers came ashore on Block Island, hence the name of this inn. The 1661 Inn is part of a complex of guesthouses. It offers spectacular views of the Atlantic Ocean from decks and verandas in the common areas and from several of the guest rooms, which are named for Block Island's founding families. Breakfast, enjoyed outdoors on warm, sunny mornings, is always served with a complimentary glass of champagne and a stunning waterfront view. In the summer season, guests are invited for an afternoon "wine and nibble hour," which features snacks and selected wines.

THE 1661 INN & HOTEL MANISSES
BLOCK ISLAND

P.O. Box 1
Block Island, RI 02807
401-466-2421
www.blockislandresorts.com

House Specialty

Baked Bluefish

This dish makes an impressive presentation on the inn's brunch buffet and makes use of the bounty of the sea enjoyed on Block Island. It's a very simple recipe that is meant to highlight the flavor of the fresh-caught fish.

On Block Island, large bluefish are not hard to come by, and the chef at the 1661 Inn usually bakes a ten-pound bluefish to serve at the inn's seaside buffet.

Baked Bluefish

Yields 8 to 10 servings

1 carrot, chopped coarse

1 small yellow onion, chopped fine

Salt and pepper

1 5-pound whole bluefish, gutted

Roasted vegetables, for serving

1. Preheat the oven to 350°F. Grease a 15 x 9-inch baking sheet with sides.

2. Mix the carrots and onions together and season with salt and pepper.

3. Stuff the cavity of the fish with the chopped carrots and onions.

4. Place the stuffed fish, with the cavity facing down, on the baking sheet. (The onions and carrots will be touching the baking sheet.) Do not bake the fish on its side.

5. Bake for about 45 minutes, or until the skin turns crispy.

6. Transfer to a platter and serve with roasted vegetables.

Local Color

The names of the 1661 Inn and its sister property, Hotel Manisses, reflect the island's history. 1661 is the year that the island was settled after being discovered by Adrian Block, a Dutch explorer who landed on the island in 1614 and named it after himself. *Manisses*, meaning "Island of the Little God," was the name originally given to the island by its earlier inhabitants, the Narragansett Indians.

Bike Around the Island

Cars are allowed but not really necessary for a short stay on this pork-chop-shaped island, which is only about six miles long and three and a half miles wide. Bikes are an ideal mode of transportation and offer splendid views of the varied shoreline beaches and cliffs. The Nature Conservancy has included Block Island in its original list of twelve "Last Great Places" in the Western Hemisphere, and more than 43 percent of the island has been set aside for conservation.

There are multiple places to rent bikes on the island, or you can bring your own on the ferry. For a comprehensive Block Island bike tour itinerary, take a look at the one put together by Tom Brosnahan of New England Travel Planner: www.newenglandtravelplanner.com/go/ri/block_island/sights/bike_itin.html. Sites not to miss include the 150-foot-high Mohegan Bluffs, Southeast and North Lighthouses, Rodman's Hollow, Clayhead Nature Trail, and Settler's Rock.

EDGEWOOD MANOR

This circa 1905 Greek Revival mansion was originally commissioned by Samuel Priest, a wealthy businessman. Over the years, it was a convent, a hospital, and a rooming house before it was restored to its original grandeur in 1994. The inn boasts many period details, such as leaded- and stained-glass windows and ornate fireplaces. Nestled between Narragansett Bay and the 435-acre Roger Williams Park, the inn is two and a half miles from downtown Providence, a city rich in history and the arts.

232 Norwood Avenue
Providence, RI 02905
401-781-0099
www.providence-lodging.com

House Specialty

Eggs Florentine

This recipe comes from a chef at a bed and breakfast
in Italy, where the innkeeper stayed many years ago.

Local Color

Known as the Ocean State, Rhode Island has over
400 miles of scenic coastline and more than a hundred public
and private beaches. Go to www.visitrhodeisland.com/
what-to-do/beaches/ for a complete list of beaches
(and the facilities offered) broken down by area.

Eggs Florentine

Yields 2 servings

4 to 6 large eggs

2 tablespoons salted butter

2 tablespoons chopped chives

¼ cup spinach leaves, washed

¼ cup cream cheese, cut into
    small cubes

1. Whisk the eggs and ¼ cup of water together in a small bowl.

2. Melt the butter in a skillet over medium heat.

3. Add the chives and sauté for about 2 minutes.

4. Add the spinach and sauté another 1 or 2 minutes.

5. Pour the egg mixture into the pan and, using a spatula, gently begin to scramble the eggs.

6. When the eggs are about three-quarters done, add the cream cheese.

7. Continue cooking just until the cream cheese melts, about 2 minutes.

Local Color

For the smallest state in the country, Rhode Island has had more than its share of "firsts." Among its claims to fame: The first polo match played in the United States, the first open golf tournament, the first National Lawn Tennis Championship, the first circus in the U.S., and the first Afro-American regiment to fight for America against the British in the Battle of Rhode Island during the Revolutionary War.

Things to Do

Experience WaterFire Providence

One of the most unique and powerful works of installation art in New England is WaterFire Providence. On WaterFire evenings, 100 bonfires are set alight just above the waters of the Woonasquatucket, Moshassuck, and Providence Rivers in the middle of downtown Providence, turning the city into a living work of art. Originally created by Barnaby Evans in 1994 to commemorate the tenth anniversary celebration of First Night Providence, the exhibition has gained the support of ardent art lovers and has evolved into a permanent event.

Today, WaterFire relies on hundreds of volunteers to tend the fires. Music from around the world plays all along the Riverwalk, creating an unforgettable experience that engages all the senses. You can view WaterFire on foot or by gondola. Nearly two million visitors from around the world come to witness this incredible spectacle. Visit www.waterfire.org for more information and a schedule of WaterFire evenings.

THE PILLSBURY HOUSE

Built in 1875, the Pillsbury House features the original intricate parquet floors and high ceilings. Located in Woonsocket's North End Historic District, the inn is a half-mile from the Blackstone River, which is credited with powering the birth of the American Industrial Revolution. Guests can enjoy the natural beauty of the area with its outdoor activities, explore the many historic sites in the Blackstone River Valley, visit New England's largest zoo in nearby Mendon, Massachusetts — or just enjoy a sherry by the fireplace or curl up with a good book on the inn's shaded porch.

Pillsbury House
Bed & Breakfast

341 Prospect Street
Woonsocket, RI 02895
401-766-7983
www.pillsburyhouse.com

House Specialty

Apple Pancakes

Except for the olive oil, all the ingredients for this recipe come from Rhode Island. The apples are from a tree in the backyard of the inn.

Tasty Tidbit

Gristmills, like the one that produces the pancake mix used in the Pillsbury House's Apple Pancakes, were once plentiful in Rhode Island, in part because water-powered mills that were used for other area industries could also be used for grinding wheat and corn.

Apple Pancakes

Yields 12 small pancakes

1¼ cups apple and spice pancake mix (innkeeper's preference: Kenyon's Grist Mill Apples & Spice Pancake Mix)

3 tablespoons olive oil

1 large egg

1 cup apple juice

2 medium apples, peeled and thinly sliced into 6 slices each

Sliced strawberries, for garnish

1. Combine the pancake mix, olive oil, egg, and apple juice and mix well.

2. Grease and heat a griddle to 380°F.

3. Drop spoonfuls of batter onto the hot griddle and cook until puffed and full of bubbles.

4. Gingerly place one apple slice, whole or cut up, onto the center of each pancake and spoon a little batter over it to cover.

5. Cook 30 seconds more, then carefully flip and cook another 1 to 2 minutes, or until done.

6. Garnish with sliced strawberries and serve.

Tasty Tidbit

The Pillsbury House innkeeper gets the apple juice for this recipe from Phantom Farms in Cumberland, Rhode Island. A family-run farm, it has been in operation for the past sixty years, growing over fifteen varieties of apples. In addition to apples, the farm grows a variety of fruits and vegetables. There's also a bakery and gift shop that features other local Rhode Island products.

Explore the History of Industry

The Blackstone River Valley, a National Heritage Corridor, contains more than 10,000 historic sites and buildings. The Blackstone River flows from Worcester, Massachusetts, to Providence, Rhode Island, and served as the power source for the Slater Mill in Pawtucket, Rhode Island. Built in 1790, it was the first successful cotton-spinning mill in America. Historians say this was the country's turning point from farm to factory, earning the Blackstone River Valley the designation of "The Birthplace of the American Industrial Revolution." Visit the National Park website (www.nps.gov/blac/index.htm) to learn more and plan your own tour of this historically rich area.

The Slater Mill (top) and the Sylvanus Brown House (bottom) are part of the Slater Mill Historic Site, and contain exhibits that show cotton spinning pre- and post-Industrial Revolution.

THE TOWER HOUSE

The historic Pier section of Narragansett, where the Tower House is located, was a premier resort destination during the late 1800s. A casino, ballrooms, a bandstand, tennis courts, bowling, and all manner of diversions attracted distinguished visitors and socialites looking for a glamorous summer holiday. Some of the best beaches in New England are within walking distance of the inn.

46 Earles Court
Narragansett, RI 02882
401-783-3787
www.towerhousebandb.com

House Specialties

Jonnycakes

This recipe comes from the Samuel E. Perry Grist Mill, which was originally built in 1703. It is the only water-powered working mill currently operating in Rhode Island and is open for tours by appointment; call: 401-783-5483.

Tower House French Toast

This "French toast" has a custardy, flan-like consistency. For a flavor variation, try substituting croissants or raisin bread for the hoagie rolls.

Jonnycakes

Yields 10 to 12 3-inch pancakes

1 tablespoon granulated sugar

½ teaspoon salt

1 cup Rhode Island Jonnycake
  White Flint Cornmeal from
  Samuel E. Perry Grist Mill
  (or other jonnycake cornmeal)

1 cup boiling water

¾ tablespoon whole milk,
  plus more as needed

Salted butter, for serving

1. Combine the sugar, salt, and cornmeal in a large mixing bowl.

2. Pour in the boiling water and stir well.

3. Immediately add the milk to thin the mixture enough to drop easily from a spoon. (Additional milk may be necessary—the mixture should be the consistency of thin mashed potatoes.)

4. Heat a griddle to medium-hot and grease with bacon grease or corn oil (do not let the griddle get dry). Drop the batter by the spoonful onto the griddle

5. Cook 5 to 6 minutes on each side, or until a crunchy brown crust forms on the outside and the inside is soft.

6. Serve the jonnycakes hot with a pat of butter.

■ ■ ■ ■ ■ ■ ■ ■ ■ ■ ■ ■

Tasty Tidbit

Rhode Island claims to be the state of origin for jonnycakes, which were passed on to early European settlers by Native Americans. There are two theories on how the cakes got their name: one is from the word *joniken*, which is the Native American word for cornmeal cakes. Others believe that the cake's portability gave it the name *journey cake*, which eventually became jonnycake.

■ ■ ■ ■ ■ ■ ■ ■ ■ ■ ■ ■

Tower House French Toast

Yields 8 to 12 servings

½ cup (1 stick) salted butter

1½ cups dark brown sugar, packed

2 to 3 submarine sandwich or hoagie rolls, sliced ½ to ¾ inch thick

6 large eggs

1½ cups whole milk

1 to 2 teaspoons cinnamon (enough to cover top of casserole)

1. Preheat the oven to 350°F.

2. Melt the butter in the bottom of a 13 x 9-inch baking dish.

3. Sprinkle the sugar over the melted butter to cover the bottom of the baking dish.

4. Place the roll slices, flat-side down, on top of the sugar and butter.

5. Whisk the eggs and milk together in a medium bowl.

6. Pour the egg mixture over the bread and let soak for 15 minutes.

7. Sprinkle cinnamon on top of the mixture.

8. Bake for ½ hour, or until puffed up.

9. Spoon a portion onto each plate and drizzle with syrup from the baking dish.

Coffee Milk

This signature Rhode Island beverage was introduced sometime in the early 1930s and declared the official state drink in 1993. Legend has it that a creative counter operator in a drugstore diner sweetened leftover coffee grounds with milk and sugar and created a syrup that is added to milk, much like chocolate syrup. Today, there is only one manufacturer of coffee syrup, Autocrat. Try a glass: Mix 2 tablespoons of coffee syrup to 8 ounces of milk.

VICTORIAN LADIES INN

This inn was originally built in 1855 on the first gaslit street in America and is included in the National Register of Historic Places. The property consists of three guesthouses connected with walkways and gardens. It's a short walk to the harbor and Newport's famous mansions.

63 Memorial Boulevard
Newport, RI 02840
1-888-849-9960
www.victorianladies.com

House Specialties

Eggs Newport

The bounty of the Rhode Island shoreline and the richness of the
Golden Age of Newport come together in this indulgent breakfast dish,
featuring crab cakes with poached eggs and aioli sauce.

Honey's Crumb Cake

This often-requested recipe offers fantastic flavor with a shortcut:
It starts with a mix, but no one will ever guess!

Local Color

The oldest tavern in America is Newport's White Horse Tavern
(www.whitehorsenewport.com). It opened in 1673, and through
its doors have passed soldiers, pirates, businessmen, and many
other famous and common folk in search of libation. The tavern's
name harks back to its early days, when many people couldn't
read. Instead of words, symbols were used for identification, and
the symbol for a tavern was a white horse.

Eggs Newport

Yields 5 servings

½ pound canned premium crabmeat

Splash of lemon juice

½ tablespoon Dijon mustard

1 tablespoon mayonnaise

½ tablespoon chopped fresh Italian parsley

10 Ritz crackers, crushed

12 large eggs, divided

1½ teaspoons Old Bay seasoning

Up to 1 teaspoon cayenne pepper, according to taste

1 roasted red pepper, chopped fine, plus more for garnish

1 scallion, green and white parts chopped fine (optional)

1 tablespoon vinegar

Aioli Sauce (below), for drizzling

Parsley and slices of fruit and tomatoes, for garnish (optional)

1. Combine the crabmeat, lemon juice, mustard, mayonnaise, parsley, crackers, 2 eggs, Old Bay seasoning, cayenne pepper, red pepper, and scallions, if using, in a bowl and mix well.

2. Form the mixture into 5 crab cakes, shaped into approximately 3-inch ovals (large enough to fit 2 eggs on top of each one).

3. Coat a medium skillet with vegetable cooking spray and place over medium-high heat. Brown the crab cakes about 3 minutes per side.

4. While the crab cakes are browning, poach 10 eggs: Put the vinegar and 4 quarts of water in a large stockpot over high heat. Once the water is boiling, crack the eggs into a cup, one at a time, and gently slide into the water. (You can poach up to 4 eggs at a time.) Once the egg forms its shape and floats to the top, about 4 minutes, remove from the pot with a slotted spoon.

5. Place 2 poached eggs on top of each crab cake and drizzle a spoonful of aioli over the top. Garnish with a little roasted red pepper. Add parsley and slices of fruit and tomato, if desired.

Aioli Sauce

A plastic squeeze bottle like the kind used to hold ketchup and mustard at restaurants works well as a container for this sauce and makes it easy to drizzle it on top of the crab cakes and poached eggs.

Yields about 2 cups

1½ cups mayonnaise

2 tablespoons roasted red peppers, chopped fine

2 teaspoons Dijon mustard

2 teaspoons finely chopped chives

1. Whisk all the ingredients together. The mixture should be on the thick side but still runny enough to drizzle on top of the eggs and crab cakes. Cover leftovers and store in the refrigerator for up to 2 weeks.

Honey's Crumb Cake

Yields 16 slices

1 box (16½ ounces) yellow cake mix (innkeeper's preference: Duncan Hines Classic Yellow Cake Mix)

1½ cups (3 sticks) salted butter, melted

1 cup granulated sugar

3 cups all-purpose flour

2 teaspoons vanilla extract

2 teaspoons cinnamon

Confectioners' sugar, for garnish

1. Preheat the oven to 350°F.

2. Prepare the cake mix according to the package directions and pour it into a greased 13 x 9-inch glass baking dish.

3. Bake for 18 minutes.

4. While the cake is baking, make the topping. Put the butter, sugar, flour, vanilla, and cinnamon into a bowl and mix well with a fork or with your hands to form medium-sized crumbs.

5. Crumble the topping on the cake.

6. Bake for an additional 18 to 20 minutes, or until lightly browned on top.

7. Cool completely, 1 to 2 hours, on a cooling rack, then sift confectioners' sugar on top.

WILLIAM'S GRANT INN

This handsome five-bay Federal-style home was built in 1808 as the residence of sea captain and shipowner William Bradford III, grandson of Deputy Governor William Bradford. Through the next 150 years, the house was inhabited by several generations of the Bradford family. It has been welcoming guests as a bed and breakfast since 1993.

154 High Street
Bristol, RI 02809
401-253-4222
www.williamsgrantinn.com

House Specialties

Egg Soufflé

Prep this recipe the night before you're going to serve it.
This allows the flavors a chance to develop and gives you
more time to spend with your guests in the morning.

Wild Blueberry Stuffed French Toast

This is a delicious summertime treat when wild blueberries are in season, but you
can make it with frozen blueberries at other times of the year.

Cranberry-Cream Cheese Muffins

The cream cheese in the batter gives these muffins an extra-rich flavor.

*Each guest room in William's Grant Inn has its own theme related to local history. The
Nautical Room is in honor of the area's maritime history and the America's Cup Hall of
Fame in Bristol; the Sturbridge Room gives a nod to Old Sturbridge Village, a living museum
depicting early American life; and the Blithewold Room recognizes the mansion and gardens
built by Augustus Van Wickle and his wife, Bessie Pardee Van Wickle (see page 77).*

Egg Soufflé

Yields 8 to 10 servings

Note advance prep time.

10 large eggs

1½ teaspoons dry mustard

½ teaspoon salt

3 cups half-and-half

3 to 4 slices Rhode Island
Portuguese sweet bread (or
other sweet bread), torn into
½-inch cubes

1 pound very sharp cheddar
cheese (innkeeper's preference:
Really-Aged Cheddar Cheese
from Harmon's General Store in
Sugar Hill, New Hampshire)

Orange, strawberry, and avocado
slices and parsley sprigs, for
garnish

1. Using a food processor, thoroughly mix the eggs, mustard, and salt.

2. Mix in the half-and-half and set aside.

3. Cover the bottom of a 12 x 9-inch baking dish with the bread cubes.

4. Grate the cheese over the bread.

5. Pour the egg mixture over the bread and cheese.

6. Cover and refrigerate overnight.

7. In the morning, preheat the oven to 350°F.

8. Bake the soufflé for 45 to 50 minutes (in a convection oven; may take a little longer in a conventional oven), or until the top is golden brown.

9. Cool the soufflé for 10 minutes, then slice it into squares and garnish each square with orange, strawberry, and avocado slices and top with a sprig of parsley.

Tasty Tidbit

Rhode Island has something of a reputation for its Portuguese sweet bread
(used in the Egg Soufflé and Wild Blueberry Stuffed French Toast recipes). According
to the Amaral family, one of the best-known bakers of the bread, Portuguese sweet bread
was created in 1863 on the island of São Miguel (that's St. Michael to Americans) in
Portugal's Azores and eventually brought to Rhode Island and Massachusetts. Some
landmark purveyors of the sweet bread include Amaral's Bakery in Warren, Rhode Island,
and Fall River, Massachusetts, and the Silver Star Bakery, Wayland Bakery, and
Taunton Avenue Bakery, all in Providence, Rhode Island.

Wild Blueberry Stuffed French Toast

Yields 8 to 12 servings

Note advance prep time.

12 large eggs

⅓ cup grade B maple syrup

2 cups 1% milk or half-and-half

4 to 5 slices Rhode Island Portuguese sweet bread (or other sweet bread), torn into ½-inch cubes

1 pound cream cheese, cut into ½-inch cubes

1½ cups wild blueberries, fresh or frozen (but not thawed)

Blueberry Sauce (below), for drizzling

1. Combine the eggs, maple syrup, and milk and mix well.

2. Coat a 13 x 9-inch baking pan with vegetable cooking spray. Cover the bottom with cubes of sweet bread.

3. Spread the cubes of cream cheese over the bread pieces.

4. Sprinkle the blueberries over the cream cheese and bread.

5. Cover with an additional layer of bread cubes.

6. Stir the egg mixture to be sure the syrup is mixed in, then pour it over the bread mixture.

7. Cover the pan with foil and refrigerate overnight.

8. In the morning, preheat the oven to 350°F.

9. Bake the French toast for 30 minutes (in a convection oven; may take a little longer in a conventional oven), then remove the foil and bake for 30 minutes more.

10. Cut the French toast into squares and drizzle with warm blueberry sauce.

Blueberry Sauce

Yields about 3 cups

2 cups granulated sugar

1 teaspoon cinnamon

4 tablespoons cornstarch

1 cup orange juice

2 cups wild blueberries, fresh or frozen

1. Mix the sugar, cinnamon, and cornstarch together in a large saucepan.

2. Add 1 cup of water and the orange juice and heat over medium heat, stirring occasionally, until warm, about 5 to 8 minutes.

3. Add the blueberries and bring to a slow boil, stirring occasionally, until the berries have burst, about 5 minutes.

4. To achieve the desired consistency, add more water to make it thinner or more cornstarch to make it thicker.

Cranberry-Cream Cheese Muffins

Yields 10 to 12 muffins

2 cups all-purpose flour

1½ teaspoons baking powder

½ teaspoon salt

¾ cup chopped pecans

1 cup salted butter, softened

8 ounces cream cheese,
  at room temperature

4 large eggs

2 teaspoons vanilla extract

1½ cups granulated sugar

2 cups cranberries, fresh or frozen
  (not thawed)

1. Preheat the oven to 350°F.

2. Mix the flour, baking powder, salt, and pecans together in a large bowl and set aside.

3. In a mixer, combine the butter, cream cheese, eggs, vanilla, and sugar.

4. Place the cranberries in the large bowl with the dry ingredients and toss to coat.

5. Fold the wet mixture into the dry mixture until all of the dry ingredients are incorporated.

6. Coat the muffin tins with vegetable cooking spray. Spoon the batter into the muffin cups, filling each about three-quarters of the way.

7. Bake the muffins for about 25 minutes, or until the edges are just light brown.

8. Cool slightly, about 5 to 7 minutes, then remove the muffins from the pans to a cooling rack or serve warm.

Things to Do

Visit Blithewold Mansion, Gardens & Arboretum

Hailed as one of the top five public gardens in New England, Blithewold features water and rock gardens, rose gardens, cutting gardens, and numerous specimen trees, plus indoor exhibits and plant showings in its greenhouse. Also on the property is a forty-five-room English style manor home from the early 1900s. It contains all the furnishings and antiques of the manor's original family, the Van Wickles, with period details right down to the original wallpaper in most of the rooms, and is open for tours. Events and programs are offered year-round, including Daffodil Days in the spring, a showy display of the property's thousands of daffodils, and Christmas at Blithewold, where visitors get to to see an early twentieth-century home lavishly decorated for the holidays. Visit www.blithewold. org for more information and current program listings.

CLIFFSIDE INN

This restored 1876 Victorian manor house, steps away from the famed Cliff Walk, was once the home of artist Beatrice Turner. Although pampered with luxurious modern amenities, such as spa showers and whirlpool baths, guests will feel that they have stepped back into a bygone time of gracious refinement as they gather in the inn's elegantly decorated common rooms, relax on the verandas and wraparound porch, or stroll the walking paths through the formal perennial gardens. It's easy to see why Cliffside has been designated as one of New England's most romantic inns.

2 Seaview Avenue
Newport, RI 02840
401-847-1811
www.cliffsideinn.com

House Specialties

Lemon-Ricotta Pancakes
with Blueberry Compote

Whipped egg whites in the batter add a light touch to these flavorful pancakes.

Mixed Berry-Cheesecake French Toast

An abundance of fresh berries, half-and-half, and a touch of Chambord create an extravagant flavor, whose richness echoes the hallmark sumptuousness of the inn.

Complementing the rich and decadent fare at the Cliffside Inn is its elegant setting for dining: Breakfast, with its renowned entrées and seasonal additions, is served in the inn's grand Victorian parlor or enjoyed on the veranda on fair-weather mornings. After a day exploring Newport, guests are welcomed back to the inn with a relaxing wine and hors d'oeuvres reception.

Lemon-Ricotta Pancakes with Blueberry Compote

Yields 8 to 10 pancakes

1¼ cups all-purpose flour

1½ teaspoons baking powder

½ teaspoon nutmeg

½ teaspoon salt

6 tablespoons (¾ stick) unsalted butter

1 cup whole milk

3 large eggs, separated

2 tablespoons granulated sugar, divided

Zest of 2 lemons

3 tablespoons freshly squeezed lemon juice

½ teaspoon vanilla extract

1 cup whole-milk ricotta cheese

Blueberry Compote (page 81), for serving

Orange slices, for garnish (optional)

1. In a medium bowl, sift together the flour, baking powder, nutmeg, and salt and set aside.

2. Heat the butter and milk in a small saucepan over medium-low heat, stirring occasionally, until the butter has melted. Remove from the heat and cool slightly.

3. In a large bowl, whisk the egg yolks, 1 tablespoon of sugar, lemon zest, lemon juice, and vanilla.

4. Add a quarter of the milk and butter mixture to the egg yolk mixture and whisk (this helps prevent the eggs from curdling). Whisk in the remaining milk and butter mixture until smooth.

5. Add the flour mixture and stir with a rubber spatula until just combined—do not overmix—and set aside.

6. In a food processor, whisk the egg whites and 1 tablespoon of sugar to soft peaks. Using a rubber spatula, fold the whites into the batter until just combined.

7. Fold the ricotta gently into the batter.

8. Heat a large nonstick frying pan or griddle on medium heat.

9. Lightly coat the pan's surface with butter, then use a ¼-cup measuring cup to scoop the batter into the pan (will form approximately 3½-inch pancakes). Cook for 4 to 5 minutes, or until bubbles form on top of the pancakes. Flip the pancakes and cook the other side for another 1 or 2 minutes, or until the bottom is golden brown.

10. Spoon warm compote over the pancakes and garnish with orange slices, if desired. Serve immediately.

Blueberry Compote

The compote can be made in advance and refrigerated. Be sure to heat thoroughly prior to serving.

Yields about 2½ cups

½ cup granulated sugar

2 tablespoons cornstarch

1 tablespoon freshly
   squeezed lemon juice

2½ cups blueberries

1. In a medium pan, combine ½ cup of water with the sugar, cornstarch, and lemon juice, bring to a boil, and cook until the sugar has melted.

2. Add 1½ cups of the blueberries and boil slowly over medium heat, stirring frequently. Cook approximately 8 to 10 minutes, or until the blueberries begin to burst.

3. Add the remaining blueberries and continue to cook over medium heat for 6 to 8 minutes. The compote will be done when it coats the spoon.

Mixed Berry-Cheesecake French Toast

Yields 8 servings

Compote:

1 cup mashed strawberries

½ cup whole blueberries

½ cup whole blackberries

½ cup granulated sugar

4 tablespoons cornstarch

1 cup hot tap water

⅛ cup Chambord

French toast:

8 large eggs

1 cup granulated sugar, divided

1 cup half-and-half

1 teaspoon cinnamon

1 package (8 ounces) cream cheese, softened

1 teaspoon vanilla extract

8 thick slices challah bread, slit from the top, almost in half, to make a "pocket"

Garnish:

Fresh sliced strawberries

Confectioners' sugar

Sprigs of mint

1. Preheat the oven to 100°F.

2. Make the compote: Heat the strawberries, blueberries, blackberries, and sugar in a saucepan over medium heat.

3. While the berries and sugar are heating, mix the cornstarch and hot water together in a bowl, then stir into the berry mixture.

4. Reduce the heat to low and cook, stirring occasionally, until thickened, about 5 minutes. Stir in the Chambord and remove from the heat.

5. In a small bowl, whisk together the eggs and ¼ cup of the sugar, until light yellow. Then add the half-and-half and cinnamon and whisk until smooth. Set aside.

6. Mix together the cream cheese, vanilla, and ¾ cup of sugar in a food processor until smooth.

7. Open the "pocket" of a bread slice and spread the cream-cheese mixture inside. Repeat with the remaining bread slices.

8. Heat a little butter in a large skillet or griddle over medium heat.

9. Dip the pockets into the egg mixture and place them in the skillet.

10. Cook the pockets until golden on both sides, about 3 minutes per side.

11. Place the pan-fried pockets on a baking sheet and put in the oven to keep warm while cooking the remaining sandwiches. Add more butter to the pan as needed to prevent the sandwiches from sticking.

12. Spoon warm berry compote over the French toast and top with sliced fresh strawberries and a dusting of confectioners' sugar. Finish with a sprig of fresh mint.

Tour Newport Mansions

No visit to Newport would be complete without touring one or more of its famous mansions. Starting in the mid-1800s, prosperous northerners as well as southern plantation owners looking for an escape from the heat began constructing summer "cottages" overlooking the water in Newport. By the turn of the twentieth century, the Gilded Age was in full swing, and the list of those summering in elaborate mansions read like a "Who's Who" of America's wealthiest families. During the "season," the Vanderbilts, Astors, Wideners, and other prominent families held lavish parties, balls, and dinners. Today, many of the mansions are open for tours, and guests can catch a glimpse of a time when fashion, design, and entertaining were sumptuous beyond imagining. For an up-to-date listing of events and mansion operating hours, visit www. newportmansions.org, the Preservation Society of Newport County's Mansion web page. Another lovely way to view the mansions is to stroll the three-and-a-half-mile long Cliff Walk that meanders along the coast and passes behind many of these gorgeous homes and gardens.

OCEAN HOUSE

A testament to luxury seaside vacations since 1868, the Ocean House overlooks a long stretch of beach and boasts stunning views of the Atlantic Ocean. From the time of its opening right after the Civil War, Ocean House attracted many distinguished guests. In 1916, it was featured in the silent movie *American Aristocracy*, which starred Douglas Fairbanks. By 2003, however, the building had fallen into such disrepair that it had to be closed. Today, guests are welcomed to a new structure that retains the exterior design of the original yet provides even more luxurious accommodations.

1 Bluff Avenue
Watch Hill, RI 02891
401-584-7000
www.oceanhouseri.com

Poached Eggs over Red Flannel, Root Vegetable, and Corned Beef Hash

This flavor-rich breakfast or brunch entrée requires a bit of advance planning: The corned beef has to marinate for two days before cooking.

Lobster and Crab Benedict with Braised Prosciutto and Parsnip-Vanilla Purée

Some of New England's richest bounty from the sea is used to create this indulgent breakfast dish. It's a treat for any holiday or special occasion, but plan ahead: The prosciutto has to braise for several hours before being used in the dish.

Tasty Tidbit

Red flannel hash is a traditional New England dish usually made with the leftovers of another New England staple, the boiled dinner. Stories abound as to how it got its name—all involve throwing someone's "red flannels" into the cooking pot—but in today's recipes, the dish gets its red color from beets.

Poached Eggs over Red Flannel, Root Vegetable, and Corned Beef Hash

Yields 5 servings

Note advance prep time.

1 large red beet

1 large yellow beet

1 large Chioggia beet

3 cups salt

2 large sweet potatoes, peeled and sliced lengthwise in ¼-inch slices

12 Brussels sprouts

1 recipe Corned Beef (page 87)

2 tablespoons Worcestershire sauce

Salt and pepper

10 poached eggs (box, page 88)

1 recipe Hollandaise Sauce (page 88), for drizzling

Frisée, paper-thin radish slices, and finely chopped chives, for garnish

1. Preheat the oven to 350°F.

2. Place the red, yellow, and Chioggia beets in a baking pan and cover with the salt.

3. Wrap with aluminum foil and bake in the oven for 45 minutes.

4. Unwrap the pan and let cool for 10 minutes, then peel and dice the beets.

5. Heat a sauté pan over medium-high heat. When hot, add the beets, sweet potatoes, and Brussels sprouts and sauté until the edges turn golden.

6. Add the corned beef and Worcestershire and season with salt and pepper. Sauté for 10 minutes, stirring occasionally.

7. Once the hash is hot, place it in a bowl or on individual plates. Top each serving with 2 poached eggs. Drizzle with hollandaise sauce, garnish with frisée, radish slices, and chives, and serve.

Corned Beef

2 cups apple cider

2 cups salt

2 tablespoons pink salt (curing salt)

1 cup maple syrup

1 cup dark brown sugar, packed

8 star anise

5 cinnamon sticks

1 onion, chopped

1 bunch thyme

2 teaspoons ginger

2 garlic cloves

2 teaspoons allspice

½ teaspoon mace

1 teaspoon red pepper flakes

1 tablespoon coriander

1 3-pound beef brisket

1. Place 2 cups of water and all the ingredients except for the beef brisket into a large pot and bring to a boil. Boil for 10 minutes.

2. Remove from the heat and add 4 cups of ice to the mixture to cool it down.

3. Pour the marinade over the beef brisket and refrigerate in a covered container for 2 days.

4. After two days, discard the marinade. Place the brisket in a large pot, cover with water, and simmer for 4 hours, or until the beef begins to flake off.

5. Let the brisket cool, then dice into small cubes.

Hollandaise Sauce

2 egg yolks

3 tablespoons freshly squeezed
   Meyer lemon juice

½ cup clarified butter

2 dashes Tabasco sauce

Lemon zest, to taste

Salt and pepper

1. Combine the egg yolks and lemon juice in a medium bowl and place over a pot of simmering water or in the top of a double boiler.

2. Whisk constantly over low heat until the egg yolks thicken and form ribbons. (If the heat is too high, the eggs will scramble.)

3. Remove from the heat and drizzle a thin stream of clarified butter into the egg mixture, whisking constantly until all the butter is added and the sauce has thickened.

4. Finish by whisking in the Tabasco, lemon zest, salt, and pepper.

Poached Eggs

2 tablespoons
   Champagne vinegar

1 tablespoon salt

8 to 10 large eggs

1. Set up a tray with paper towels to drain the cooked eggs.

2. Bring 2 quarts of water, with the vinegar and salt, to a gentle simmer in a large saucepan.

3. Crack each egg into a cup or ramekin, and carefully place them in the water. Poach 3 or 4 eggs at a time, until the whites are set and opaque, 3 to 5 minutes depending on preferred doneness.

4. Remove the eggs with a slotted spoon and drain on the paper towels.

Lobster and Crab Benedict with Braised Prosciutto and Parsnip-Vanilla Purée

Yields 4 servings

Note advance prep time.

2 whole lobsters

2 tablespoons unsalted butter

12 ounces canned Jonah crab or jumbo lump crabmeat

2 cups Braised Prosciutto (page 90)

4 English muffins

8 poached eggs (box, page 88)

1 recipe Béarnaise Sauce (page 91)

1 recipe Parsnip-Vanilla Purée (page 91)

Frisée, paper-thin radish slices, and finely chopped chives, for garnish

1. Bring a large pot of water to a boil, place the lobsters in the pot, and cook for 9 minutes.

2. Remove the lobsters and place them in an ice bath to cool down.

3. Once the lobsters have cooled, crack the shells and remove and chop the lobster meat.

4. Melt the butter in a heated sauté pan over medium heat.

5. Add the lobster meat, Jonah crab, and prosciutto and cook until hot, about 5 to 7 minutes.

6. Toast the English muffins and place each one on a plate.

7. Place the lobster mixture on top of the toasted muffins.

8. Place 2 poached eggs on top of the lobster mixture on each muffin and pour Béarnaise sauce over the top.

9. Spread the purée on the side of each plate, garnish with frisée, radish slices, and chives, and serve.

Braised Prosciutto

Yields 3 cups

1 2-pound whole prosciutto

Salt and pepper

1 tablespoon vegetable oil

1 onion, diced

1 carrot, diced

2 celery stalks, diced

3 sprigs thyme

2 cups dry white wine

2 quarts chicken stock, or
    enough to cover prosciutto

1. Preheat the oven to 250°F.

2. Season the prosciutto with salt and pepper.

3. Put the oil in a medium ovenproof stockpot over medium-high heat. Add the prosciutto and brown on both sides. Remove from the pan and set aside.

4. Sweat the onion in the same pot until translucent and lightly caramelized.

5. Add the carrot, celery, and thyme and sauté for 3 to 5 minutes.

6. Deglaze the pot with white wine.

7. Return the prosciutto to the pot and cover with chicken stock. Bring to a simmer over low heat and cook for 15 minutes.

8. Cover the pot with aluminum foil and place it in the oven for 4 hours. Remove the pot from the oven and cool for about 10 minutes.

9. Shred the prosciutto and return the shredded pieces to the braising liquid until completely cooled so that it does not dry out.

10. After the prosciutto has cooled completely (about an hour), strain and discard the liquid. Place the pulled prosciutto in a bowl and set aside until ready to use.

11. Store leftover prosciutto in the refrigerator for up to 2 weeks.

Béarnaise Sauce

¼ cup chopped tarragon

2 shallots, minced

¼ cup Champagne vinegar

¼ cup white wine

3 egg yolks

½ cup (1 stick) unsalted butter, melted

Salt and pepper

3 tablespoons freshly squeezed lemon juice

1 teaspoon Tabasco sauce

1. In a small saucepan, make the Béarnaise reduction by combining the tarragon, shallots, vinegar, and wine over medium-high heat. Bring to a simmer and cook until reduced by half. Remove from the heat and set aside to cool.

2. Blend the egg yolks and Béarnaise reduction together in a blender. With the blender running, add ⅓ of the butter in a slow, steady stream. Once it emulsifies, turn the blender speed up to high and add the remaining butter.

3. Season with salt and pepper, lemon juice, and Tabasco and set aside in a warm spot (not over direct heat) to keep the sauce from separating.

Parsnip-Vanilla Purée

5 ounces parsnips, peeled and sliced

Salt and pepper

½ cup heavy cream

½ garlic clove

2 tablespoons unsalted butter

¼ vanilla bean

1. Put the parsnips in a medium saucepan. Season with salt and cover with water.

2. Place the pot over medium heat and bring to a simmer. Cook the parsnips until tender—the tip of a paring knife should easily go through without resistance—about 15 minutes.

3. Place the heavy cream and garlic in another saucepan and bring to a simmer over low heat until the cream thickens slightly, about 5 minutes. Strain and discard the garlic.

4. Drain the parsnips, reserving the cooking liquid.

5. Place the parsnips in a food processor with the butter, a couple tablespoons of the reserved cooking liquid, and the seeds scraped from the inside of the vanilla bean.

6. Begin to process and add the strained heavy cream mixture. Season with salt and pepper and purée until very smooth.

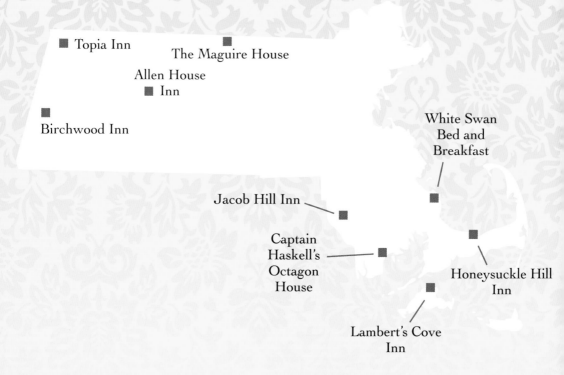

Topia Inn

The Maguire House

Allen House
Inn

Birchwood Inn

White Swan
Bed and
Breakfast

Jacob Hill Inn

Captain
Haskell's
Octagon
House

Honeysuckle Hill
Inn

Lambert's Cove
Inn

Massachusetts

By the sword we seek peace,
but peace only under liberty

—State Motto

BIRCHWOOD INN

Comfortable country elegance pervades this inn, which dates back to 1766. It's a foodie hot spot: Birchwood Inn has won numerous awards for its breakfasts as well as its accommodations. It also offers special culinary packages, including The Ultimate Chocolate Experience, An Evening with Your Personal Wine Consultant, The Brunch Bunch, and Have Your Cake and Eat It, Too. Quaint shops, the Norman Rockwell Museum, and nearby Tanglewood, where classical and contemporary music concerts are held in the summer, provide plenty of other adventures as well.

The Birchwood Inn
Fireflies and Firesides

7 Hubbard Street
Lenox, MA 01240
413-637-2600
www.birchwood-inn.com

Pear-Cranapple Crumble

This is truly a recipe for all seasons. In the summer, you can substitute peaches, nectarines, plums, and blueberries for the winter fruits used here. The topping can be made ahead of time and frozen. At Birchwood Inn, the chef makes a quadruple batch and freezes it so there's always topping on hand. If you are serving the crumble for dessert instead of breakfast, you may wish to garnish it with a dollop of ice cream or crème anglaise.

Caramel Apple Upside-Down French Toast

The aroma of the fruit baking in the oven is ambrosial, and the "upside-down" presentation is fun.

Grilled Peaches

You can substitute nectarines for the peaches in this recipe, if you wish. Grilling brings out and intensifies the intoxicating flavor of the fruit. A small scoop of tangy sorbet may be added to the center of the peach if you are serving it by itself instead of as an accompaniment.

Blueberry Sauce

Blueberry sauce is a great topping for any kind of grilled fruit as well as for blintzes, French toast, pancakes, and, of course, ice cream.

Peach Croissant French Toast Panini

The panini sandwich gets a unique twist here as a breakfast treat.

Pear-Cranapple Crumble

Yields 8 servings

Topping:

½ cup light brown sugar, packed

½ cup all-purpose flour

5 tablespoons unsalted butter, very cold, cut into large cubes

½ cup quick or old-fashioned oats

Filling:

4 apples (Cortland, Empire, or any variety suitable for baking)

2 Bosc pears

¾ cup cranberries

¼ cup honey

2 tablespoons freshly squeezed lemon juice

Fresh nutmeg, to taste

1. Combine the brown sugar, flour, and butter in a food processor and pulse until the mixture is the size of peas. Transfer to a medium bowl.

2. Stir in the oats and set aside.

3. Preheat the oven to 350°F.

4. Butter a 12 x 8-inch baking dish or 8 small individual ovenproof dishes.

5. Slice the apples and pears into ¼-inch slices and place in a medium bowl.

6. Add the cranberries.

7. Drizzle honey over the fruit.

8. Add the lemon juice and toss gently.

9. Spoon the fruit into the baking dish or dishes and cover with the topping.

10. Grate fresh nutmeg over the topping.

11. Place the baking dish or dishes in the oven and bake until the fruit is tender, 45 minutes for the baking dish; 30 minutes for the individual dishes.

■ ■ ■ ■ ■ ■ ■ ■ ■ ■ ■ ■

Tasty Tidbit

Crumble, also known as Brown Betty, has its origin in Britain and can be made in sweet or savory versions, although sweet is much more popular. Crumbles were first made during World War II, as a way of simulating pie at a time when rationed pastry ingredients were in short supply.

■ ■ ■ ■ ■ ■ ■ ■ ■ ■ ■ ■

Caramel Apple Upside-Down French Toast

Yields 8 servings

Note advance prep time.

½ cup (1 stick) unsalted butter

1 cup dark brown sugar, firmly packed

2 tablespoons light corn syrup

8 apples (Cortland, Empire, or any variety suitable for baking), cut into ½-inch slices

1 loaf challah (egg bread)

4 extra-large eggs

1 cup whole milk

1 tablespoon vanilla extract

Cinnamon sugar, for sprinkling on top

Melon slices or berries, for garnish

1. Melt the butter in a saucepan over medium-low heat.

2. Add the brown sugar and corn syrup and stir until the sugar has dissolved. Continue cooking for 3 to 5 minutes, or until the mixture is thick and bubbly.

3. Add the sliced apples, stirring gently until the all of the fruit is coated. Cook for 1 to 2 minutes.

4. Coat two 8 x 8-inch glass baking dishes with vegetable cooking spray.

5. Spread the fruit mixture evenly in the dishes.

6. Slice the top and side crusts off the challah and cut into 8 1-inch slices.

7. Place the slices in one layer on top of the fruit.

8. Cover the dishes and refrigerate overnight.

9. In the morning, remove the dishes from the refrigerator 1 hour before baking.

10. Preheat the oven to 375°F.

11. Whisk the eggs, milk, and vanilla together and pour the mixture over the bread slices.

12. Sprinkle with cinnamon sugar.

13. Bake for 60 minutes, or until the top is golden brown and crisp.

14. Remove the French toast from the oven and let sit for 5 minutes before cutting.

15. Cut the French toast into 8 servings and invert each serving on an individual plate, fruit-side up. Spoon the pan liquid over the top and garnish with colorful melon slices or berries.

Grilled Peaches

Yields 2 servings

2 ripe but firm peaches

About 4 teaspoons Blueberry
Sauce (below)

4 mint leaves, for garnish

1. Preheat a barbecue grill to medium-high (or use a grill pan on the stove).

2. Slice the peaches in half and remove the pit.

3. Coat a barbecue basket with vegetable cooking spray and place the fruit in the basket, pit-side down.

4. Put the basket on the barbecue and close the lid.

5. Grill the fruit for 5 to 8 minutes, or until the fruit is warm and there are grill marks on the top.

6. Turn the basket over, close the barbecue lid, and cook for another minute or two.

7. To serve, fill the center of each peach half with blueberry sauce and garnish with a mint leaf.

Blueberry Sauce

Yields about 1½ cups

2 cups blueberries, fresh or frozen
(preferably wild blueberries)

½ cup granulated sugar

½ tablespoon freshly squeezed
lemon juice

1½ tablespoons orange juice

2 teaspoons cornstarch

1. Combine the blueberries, sugar, and lemon juice in a medium saucepan.

2. Cook over medium heat until the sugar has dissolved and the mixture begins to boil.

3. In a small bowl, add the orange juice to the cornstarch and mix well. Stir into the berry mixture.

4. Lower the heat to medium-low and continue cooking, stirring frequently, until the sauce has thickened. Serve warm or cover and refrigerate for up to 2 weeks.

Peach Croissant French Toast Panini

Yields 6 servings

2 cups fresh strawberries, hulled and sliced

½ cup granulated sugar

8 ounces cream cheese, softened

¼ teaspoon ground ginger

¼ cup orange marmalade

¼ cup walnuts or pecans, chopped coarse

3 tablespoons Grand Marnier, divided

6 croissants

2 ripe but still firm peaches, cut into ¼-inch slices

3 large eggs

½ cup half-and-half

1 teaspoon vanilla extract

Confectioners' sugar, for garnish

1. Mix the strawberries and sugar together in a bowl and macerate for 1 hour.

2. In another bowl, mix the cream cheese, ginger, marmalade, nuts, and 2 tablespoons of Grand Marnier until mostly smooth. (This can be done a day ahead, then covered and refrigerated.)

3. Cut the croissants in half lengthwise.

4. Spread 1 to 2 tablespoons of the cream cheese mixture on the bottom half of each croissant. Top with a few peach slices. Put the croissant top back on.

5. Whisk together the eggs, half-and-half, vanilla, and 1 tablespoon of Grand Marnier in a large bowl.

6. Preheat the panini maker or griddle.

7. Dip each croissant in the egg mixture, covering all sides.

8. Grill the croissants in the panini maker until they are golden brown, and the cheese filling is soft and somewhat runny, about 2 to 3 minutes.

9. Place one croissant on each of 6 plates and top with the macerated strawberries. Sprinkle with confectioners' sugar and serve.

HONEYSUCKLE HILL INN

Listed on the National Register of Historic Places, this circa 1810 bed and breakfast has the signature design features of its time: wide-plank wood floors, ship captain's staircase, curving hallways, and a wraparound front porch that beckons guests to sit and relax. It is located on Main Street, which is part of Old King's Highway (Route 6A), one of the outstanding scenic byways in America.

591 Main Street
West Barnstable, MA 02668
508-362-8418
www.honeysucklehill.com

Ricotta-Cottage Cheese Pancakes

The inn's most-requested recipe is the one for these yummy pancakes.
They can be topped with any fresh fruit that's in season.

Mornings are a special time at Honeysuckle Hill. The coffee is always on early, and you can take a cup out on the screened-in front porch or sip it while you enjoy a stroll through the inn's lush perennial gardens. When it's time for breakfast, guests gather in the sunny dining room, which is decorated with works by local Cape Cod artists.

Ricotta-Cottage Cheese Pancakes

Yields 4 servings

1 cup unbleached white flour

1 tablespoon granulated sugar

½ teaspoon salt

1 teaspoon baking powder

4 large eggs

1 cup ricotta cheese

1 cup small-curd cottage cheese

¾ cup 2% milk

1 teaspoon vanilla extract

1 teaspoon grated lemon zest

½ teaspoon lemon extract
  (optional)

Fresh fruit of your choice and
  confectioners' sugar, for garnish

Maple syrup, for serving

1. In a medium bowl, sift together the flour, sugar, salt, and baking powder.

2. In another bowl, beat the eggs with the ricotta and cottage cheese, milk, vanilla, lemon zest, and lemon extract, if using.

3. Gradually add the wet ingredients to the dry, stirring just until blended. Do not overmix.

4. Heat a griddle to medium and lightly grease with vegetable oil. Drop a scant ¼ cup of the batter onto the griddle. Cook until the pancakes are bubbly on the top and lightly browned on the bottom, about 3 minutes. Flip them and cook 1 to 2 minutes more.

5. Top the pancakes with fresh fruit and a dusting of confectioners' sugar. Serve with local maple syrup.

Local Color

The Cape Cod National Seashore is the site of Marconi Station, where Guglielmo Marconi, an Italian inventor, engineered the first complete two-way transatlantic wireless communication in 1903. Using Morse code, a telegraph operator tapped out a message from President Theodore Roosevelt to King Edward VII in England: "In taking advantage of the wonderful triumph of scientific research and ingenuity [I extend] most cordial greetings and good wishes to you and all the people of the British Empire." Within a few hours, King Edward sent a message returning President Roosevelt's good wishes.

Things to Do

Check Out Sandy Neck Barrier Beach

Less than two miles from the inn, guests can explore 4,700 acres of shoreline ecosystems at Sandy Neck Beach Park. A barrier beach is a ridge of sand that parallels the shore but is separated from it by water or a small lagoon. Salt marshes, maritime forests, and dunes are home to numerous species of birds, including the northern harrier, American woodcock, saltmarsh sharp-tailed sparrow, and willet. There are also nine endangered species of plants, animals, and birds that can be found in the park. Designated trails allow visitors to carefully traverse this unspoiled landscape while preserving delicate habitats.

In addition to wildlife observation, Sandy Neck offers a historic lighthouse, which is not open to the public but can be seen by hiking about six miles to the tip of Sandy Neck. The 1857 lighthouse, along with antique dune shacks and cottages, have earned the park the designation of Cultural Historical District.

And, of course, there is also the option of just enjoying the sun, sand, and surf for guests who want to spend a day at the beach. Sandy Neck Beach Park has a 200-car parking lot, restrooms and changing facilities, and a concession stand. The beach is attended by a lifeguard in season (between Memorial Day and Labor Day).

JACOB HILL INN

Combining historic charm with the luxuries of a resort hotel, this bed and breakfast offers easy access to downtown Providence, Rhode Island, yet preserves the sense of a relaxing getaway on a country estate. The building is more than 290 years old and was once owned by the Jacob Hill Hunt Club, whose affluent members included the Vanderbilts, Aldriches, Firestones, and Grosvernors. Today, guests can enjoy the inground pool and tennis court or just relax and take in the view from the gazebo.

120 Jacob Street
Seekonk, MA 02771
508-336-9165
www.inn-providence-ri.com

Cinnamon-Orange Stuffed French Toast

You can serve this French toast with maple syrup if you like,
but it's sweet enough without it.

Sweet Additions

Although this recipe uses cinnamon-raisin bread and orange
marmalade, there's room for some creative variations. The
innkeeper sometimes pairs French bread with peach preserves
and warm peaches or challah bread with raspberries. If you
want to dress the dish up a bit, you can top it with a dollop of
sweetened whipped cream.

Cinnamon-Orange Stuffed French Toast

Yields 2 servings

6 slices cinnamon-swirl bread

4 ounces cream cheese (not whipped variety), softened at room temperature

3 tablespoons orange marmalade

2 large eggs

⅛ cup whole milk

½ teaspoon vanilla extract

Confectioners' sugar, orange slices, strawberry slices, and mint sprigs, for garnish

1. Spread 3 slices of bread with cream cheese.

2. Spread the other 3 slices of bread with orange marmalade.

3. Put together 1 bread slice with cream cheese and 1 slice with marmalade to make a sandwich.

4. Melt a little butter in a nonstick frying pan over medium heat or on an electric griddle set at 300°F.

5. Whisk together the eggs, milk, and vanilla.

6. Dip the sandwiches in the egg mixture and lay them on the pan or griddle. Brown each side of the sandwiches, using a spatula to flip them.

7. Cut the sandwiches on the diagonal and arrange 3 halves on each plate. Sprinkle with confectioners' sugar and garnish with orange slices, strawberry slices, and a sprig of mint.

Things to Do

Hit the Coastal Wine Trail

The Southeastern New England American Viticultural Appellation, or SENE AVA (sounds like "sea knee ava"), stretches from Cape Cod and the Islands of Massachusetts through the south coast of Massachusetts down to coastal Rhode Island and Connecticut. The Coastal Wine Trail consists of ten wineries, seven of which are not far from Jacob's Hill. What characterizes the wines of this region is the close proximity of the vineyards to the Atlantic Ocean and the southeast-facing coastline, which benefit from the warm Gulf Stream waters in the summer and fall. This cool grape-growing appellation is known for excellent white and sparkling wines.

Wine tasters can get a "passport" to take to the wineries on the Coastal Wine Trail. Visit two or more, and you can enter a year-end drawing for prizes that range from winery gift certificates to a trip. Participating wineries offer events year-round, including hay rides, jazz afternoons, and even a Wine, Cheese, and Chocolate Festival. See www.coastalwinetrail.com for a complete schedule and more information.

LAMBERT'S COVE INN

Originally a Martha's Vineyard farmhouse dating back to 1790, Lambert's Cove Inn is now a lavish country estate with elegant yet comfortably appointed guest rooms and common gathering spaces. A salt pool, spa, and tennis court are on the grounds, and the inn's private beach is a short walk away. The inn has preserved some of its original heritage, however, with a large garden that supplies fruits and vegetables for the chef's seasonal creations.

90 Manaquayak Road
Vineyard Haven, MA 02568
508-693-2298
www.lambertscoveinn.com

Cinnamon Pancakes with
Lambert's Cove Farm Apple Chutney

In a nod to the inn's early days as a farm, apples grown on a tree in the garden are picked fresh and used to make the delicious chutney topping for the pancakes.

Local Color

Martha's Vineyard is the largest island on the East Coast that is not connected to the mainland by a bridge or tunnel. Maybe that's partly why it's such a popular hideout for the rich and famous: The Kennedy family, Diane Sawyer, David Letterman, Lady Gaga, Meg Ryan, Stephen King, Carly Simon, John Belushi, Walter Cronkite, and Michael J. Fox have all been residents of the island.

Cinnamon Pancakes with Lambert's Cove Farm Apple Chutney

Yields 4 servings

2 cups all-purpose flour

2 tablespoons baking powder

1 teaspoon salt

2 tablespoons granulated sugar

2 teaspoons cinnamon

2 large eggs

1 tablespoon pure vanilla extract

1½ cups 2% milk

¼ cup (½ stick) salted butter, melted

Apple Chutney (page 111) and 2 tablespoons confectioners' sugar, for garnish

1. Mix together the flour, baking powder, salt, sugar, and cinnamon in a medium bowl. Set aside.

2. In another bowl, whisk the eggs, vanilla, milk, and butter.

3. Gently add the flour mixture to the egg mixture until just incorporated (it may still contain some lumps). Let sit for 5 minutes.

4. Heat a skillet on medium heat and grease with 1 tablespoon of oil.

5. Ladle the pancake batter onto the skillet in 4-inch rounds and cook until golden brown, about 2 minutes. Flip the pancakes and cook for another 2 minutes. Repeat with the remaining batter, using additional oil to grease the skillet as needed.

6. Serve immediately, topped with apple chutney and confectioners' sugar.

Apple Chutney

Yields about 2½ cups

2 tablespoons vegetable oil

½ cup minced onions

2 tablespoons salted butter

2 cups diced farm-fresh apples

1 teaspoon allspice

1 teaspoon cinnamon

¼ cup balsamic vinegar

6 tablespoons pure maple syrup

6 tablespoons chopped walnuts

1. Heat a heavy saucepan on medium-high. Add the vegetable oil and onions. Cook for 1½ minutes, stirring often.

2. Add the butter, apples, allspice, and cinnamon and continue cooking for 2 minutes.

3. Reduce the heat to medium-low. Add the balsamic vinegar and maple syrup. Continue cooking, stirring often, until the mixture thickens and starts to caramelize—you'll hear the sizzling in the pan get louder.

4. Add the walnuts and continue cooking for another 2 minutes, stirring often; be careful not to let the mixture burn.

5. Transfer the chutney to a bowl and either serve immediately or cool and refrigerate in an airtight container for up to 1 week.

CAPTAIN HASKELL'S OCTAGON HOUSE

Originally built for Fordyce Dennis Haskell, captain of a New Bedford whaler, and his wife, Sylvia, this B&B allows guests the opportunity to experience firsthand one of the more curious fads of American architecture: the octagonal house. This style enjoyed a brief heyday from 1848 to 1860. It was popularized by pop psychologist/phrenologist Orson Squire Fowler, who claimed that octagonal houses not only featured efficient use of space and superior ventilation but also promoted health, happiness, and sexual harmony. Many original details have been preserved in the restoration of the Octagon House, including Staffordshire-tile hearths, oak parquet floors, carved papyrus-leaf door casings, and a spiral staircase.

347 Union Street
New Bedford, MA 02740
508-999-3933
www.theoctagonhouse.com

Captain Haskell's Octagon House Cranberry-Walnut Scones

These scones are best enjoyed within an hour of coming out of the oven.
They can be warmed in a 190°F oven to restore freshness,
but be careful not to dry them out.

Tasty Tidbit

American whalers and mariners
took cranberries on their voyages
to prevent scurvy.

Captain Haskell's Octagon House Cranberry-Walnut Scones

Yields 8 scones

1 cup whole wheat pastry flour

1 cup all-purpose wheat flour

2 teaspoons granulated sugar

2 teaspoons baking powder

½ teaspoon baking soda

½ teaspoon salt

¼ cup cultured buttermilk powder (innkeeper's preference: SACO)

1 tablespoon ground flaxseed meal

6 tablespoons vegetable margarine, cold

½ to ¾ cup walnuts, chopped medium

½ cup dried cranberries, chopped coarse if large

¾ cup orange juice (innkeeper's preference: Tropicana)

2 to 3 teaspoons cranberry conserve (innkeeper's preference: Trappist)

1. Preheat a convection oven to 425°F (or a conventional oven to 450°F). Lightly oil a baking sheet or coat it with vegetable cooking spray.

2. Mix the flours, sugar, baking powder, baking soda, salt, buttermilk powder, and flaxseed meal in a medium bowl.

3. Using a pastry blender or knives, cut in the margarine until the dough is the size of small peas.

4. Mix in the walnuts and cranberries.

5. Add the orange juice. Working quickly with a spatula, incorporate all the dry ingredients and form a ball of dough. Add a little extra orange juice if necessary.

6. Turn out the dough onto a well-floured board. Flour your hands and knead the dough by folding it into thirds and turning the dough for about 15 seconds, just until the dough becomes smooth and soft but not too elastic, about 6 to 10 folds. Overkneading will toughen the scones.

7. Pat the dough into a ¾-inch-thick rectangle. Thinly spread the cranberry conserves on half the dough. Fold the dough over and pat it into a rectangle approximately ½ to ¾ inch thick.

8. With a sharp knife, cut the dough first into quarters and then diagonally into eight triangles to form the scones. Arrange the scones ½ inch apart on the baking sheet.

9. Bake until lightly browned, about 8 to 9 minutes in a convection oven (or about 10 to 11 minutes in a conventional oven). Remove the scones to a cooling rack and let sit for a few minutes before serving.

Things to Do

Tour a Cranberry Bog

The cranberry is the number one agricultural commodity crop and the official state fruit of Massachusetts. There are 14,000 acres of active cranberry bogs in the state, which is the second largest grower of cranberries in the the country.

Native Americans introduced the Pilgrims to the cranberry. The fruit, native to the northern United States and Canada, was prized not only as food but also for its healing qualities and as a dye. The Pilgrims called the fruit *craneberry* because they thought the plant's flower looked like the forehead of a sandhill crane.

Contrary to popular belief, cranberries are not grown in water, but they are sometimes collected in water through a flooding process called a wet harvest. Several cranberry farms in the state offer tours (including nearby Flax Pond Farms in Carver, Massachusetts; www.flaxpondfarms.com) and even the chance to get into a cranberry bog and see for yourself how the fruit is grown.

To learn more about the cranberry's history, uses, and growing methods and for information on farms in the state that offer tours, visit www.cranberries.org.

ALLEN HOUSE INN

The Allen House, built in 1886, is one of the finest remaining examples of the stick style of architecture, which was popular from about 1860 to 1890. The style is characterized by asymmetrical forms, steeply pitched gable roofs with overhanging eaves and exposed rafter tails, and clapboard walls overlaid with decorative "stick work," or raised boards in vertical, horizontal, or diagonal patterns meant to represent the underlying structure of the house. The original six-color paint scheme on the exterior of the Allen House was faithfully restored, accenting the architectural details of the inn.

599 Main Street
Amherst, MA 01002
413-253-5000
www.allenhouse.com

Banana-Cinnamon Pancakes

These pancakes, with their soft and creamy banana filling and homey cinnamon flavor, are the ultimate in simple breakfast comfort food.

Easy Applesauce-Cinnamon Bundt Cake

Here's a great "busy day" cake that's bursting with homemade flavor.

Tasty Tidbit

Boston cream pie is the official state dessert of Massachusetts. Not really a pie at all, it's a two-layered sponge cake filled with custardy cream and frosted with chocolate. Chef M. Sanzian at Boston's Parker House Hotel is credited with its creation in 1856. Boston cream pie is thought to have been a variation of pudding pie, a popular early American dessert—and some say that's why it's called pie and not cake.

Banana-Cinnamon Pancakes

Yields about 2 dozen 4-inch pancakes

1½ cups all-purpose flour

3½ teaspoons baking powder

1 teaspoon salt

1 tablespoon granulated sugar

1¼ cups whole milk

1 extra-large egg

3 tablespoons salted or unsalted
    butter, melted

2 ripe bananas

1 tablespoon cinnamon

Banana slices, for garnish

1. Sift the flour, baking powder, salt, and sugar into a large bowl.

2. Add the milk, egg, and butter. Mix until smooth.

3. In a separate bowl, smash the bananas and add the cinnamon.

4. Blend the bananas and cinnamon into the batter.

5. Pour enough batter onto a hot griddle to make 4-inch pancakes. Cook 2 to 3 minutes until lots of bubbles form, then flip and cook a minute more.

6. Garnish with banana slices.

Easy Applesauce-Cinnamon Bundt Cake

Yields 15 to 20 slices

1 box (21.41 ounces) carrot cake
mix (innkeeper's preference:
Duncan Hines)

2 extra-large eggs

1½ cups chunky
cinnamon applesauce

¼ cup cinnamon

1. Preheat the oven to 350°F. Spray a Bundt pan with vegetable cooking spray.

2. Pour the cake mix into a bowl. Add the eggs and cinnamon applesauce and blend well.

3. Pour half of the mixture into the Bundt pan. Sprinkle half the cinnamon on top of the mixture. Carefully pour in the remaining cake mix and top with the remaining cinnamon.

4. Bake for 45 minutes, or until the cake is firm. Turn out of the pan when cool.

Things to Do

Visit the Home of an American Poet

Amherst was home to poet Emily Dickinson and features a museum (www.emilydickinsonmuseum.org) dedicated to her. The museum consists of two historic houses, The Homestead, which was the birthplace and home of Dickinson, and The Evergreens, next door, which was the home of her brother, Austin, and his family. Several guided tours are offered, presenting Emily Dickinson's story from a variety of perspectives. Interesting to note: Although Dickinson wrote nearly 1,800 poems, less than a dozen were actually published during her lifetime.

THE MAGUIRE HOUSE

Surrounded by over 40 private bucolic acres, the Maguire House offers guests spectacular views of nearby Upper Naukeag Lake and New Hampshire's Mount Monadnock, about a twenty-minute drive away. Built in 1764, the B&B was one of Ashburnham's first inns. It continued to welcome travelers for over 130 years before becoming a private residence. Since 1996, the innkeepers have returned the Maguire House to its former ways of hospitality. Amenities include fresh flowers, gourmet chocolates, spa bathrobes, and fluffy down comforters in every guest room.

30 Cobb Road
Ashburnham, MA 01430
978-827-5053
www.maguirehouse.com

House Specialties

Blueberry Buckle Muffins

A buckle is a dessert that consists of a rich cake batter with fresh
seasonal fruit mixed in and a streusel topping. Although details of the buckle's
exact origin are murky, it is thought to have been developed by the colonists
and has always been a very popular sweet in New England. This dish
is usually served in a large baking dish, so having one of these
muffins is like having your own individual buckle.

Oatmeal-Apple-Walnut Pancakes

You can leave the nuts out of this recipe if need be, but they
complement the apples very nicely in both flavor and texture.

Pumpkin Waffles

Pumpkins have come by their association with Thanksgiving honestly.
They were introduced to the Pilgrims by Native Americans
and became an important source of food for the settlers.

Poached Pears with Cranberry Compote

This breakfast fruit dish is lovely in both taste and color, and although
it seems to be a bridge between late summer and fall flavors,
the ingredients are readily available year-round.

Blueberry Buckle Muffins

Yields 12 muffins

Batter:

2 cups all-purpose flour

2 teaspoons baking powder

½ teaspoon salt

½ cup granulated sugar

1 large egg, slightly beaten

½ cup 2% milk

½ cup sour cream

⅓ cup (⅔ stick) salted butter,
   melted

1½ cups fresh blueberries, washed

Topping:

⅓ cup granulated sugar

⅓ cup all-purpose flour

¼ teaspoon salt

¼ teaspoon cinnamon

3 tablespoons salted butter,
   softened

1. Preheat the oven to 400°F. Lightly grease a 12-cup muffin tin.

2. Sift together the flour, baking powder, salt, and sugar.

3. Stir in the egg, milk, sour cream, and butter just until blended. Do not overmix.

4. Gently fold in the blueberries.

5. Combine all the topping ingredients in a small bowl and mix until crumbly.

6. Fill each muffin cup three-quarters full with batter and sprinkle the topping mixture over the muffins.

7. Bake for about 20 minutes, or until a toothpick inserted in the center comes out clean.

Oatmeal-Apple-Walnut Pancakes

Yields 6 to 8 pancakes

1½ cups buttermilk

¼ cup 2% milk

1 cup quick-cooking oatmeal

1 cup all-purpose flour

2 tablespoons light brown sugar

1½ teaspoons baking powder

¾ teaspoon baking soda

¼ teaspoon salt

3 tablespoons salted butter

1 apple, peeled, cored, and
  chopped fine

½ teaspoon cinnamon

¼ teaspoon nutmeg

2 large eggs, beaten

½ cup chopped walnuts

Warm maple syrup, for serving

1. Combine the buttermilk, milk, and oatmeal in a small bowl and let sit for 10 minutes.

2. In a large bowl, combine the flour, sugar, baking powder, baking soda, and salt.

3. Melt the butter in a small saucepan over low heat.

4. Add the apple, cinnamon, and nutmeg. Gently sauté until the apple is slightly softened, 2 to 5 minutes, depending on the firmness of the apple.

5. Stir the oatmeal mixture into the large bowl of dry ingredients and mix well.

6. Add the apple mixture and mix well.

7. Stir in the eggs.

8. Add the walnuts.

9. Heat a well-greased griddle to medium-high heat. Drop ¼ cup of the batter onto the hot griddle and cook for 1 to 2 minutes, or until bubbles form and the edges are dry. Flip the pancake and cook another 2 to 3 minutes, until browned. Repeat with the remaining batter.

10. Serve the pancakes with warm maple syrup.

Pumpkin Waffles

Yields 12 4-inch waffles

2½ cups all-purpose flour

⅓ cup light brown sugar, packed

2¼ teaspoons baking powder

1 teaspoon baking soda

½ teaspoon salt

2 teaspoons cinnamon

1 teaspoon ground ginger

¼ teaspoon ground cloves

4 large eggs

1 cup whole milk

1 cup buttermilk, well shaken

1 cup canned solid-pack pumpkin

6 tablespoons (¾ stick) unsalted butter, melted

Whole strawberries, for garnish (optional)

Warm maple syrup, for serving

1. Preheat the oven to 250°F. Preheat a Belgian waffle iron and lightly brush with vegetable oil.

2. Sift together the flour, sugar, baking powder, baking soda, salt, cinnamon, ginger, and cloves in a medium bowl.

3. Whisk the eggs in a large bowl until blended, then whisk in the milk, buttermilk, pumpkin, and butter until smooth.

4. Whisk the dry ingredients into the egg mixture just until smooth.

5. Spoon the batter (about 2 cups for 4 4-inch Belgian waffles) into the waffle iron, spreading quickly. Cook according to manufacturer's directions.

6. Transfer the waffles to a rack in the oven to keep them warm and crisp until ready to serve.

7. Garnish with strawberries, if desired, and serve with warm maple syrup.

■ ■ ■ ■ ■ ■ ■ ■ ■ ■ ■

Tasty Tidbit

Pumpkin was prized by the early colonial settlers because it was highly nutritious and kept well into the winter months. What's more, this versatile gourd was used in its entirety: The flesh was roasted, baked, boiled, and dried. The pumpkin seeds were dried and roasted and used for food and as medicine. The blossoms were added to stews, and dried pumpkin could be ground into flour. The early version of pumpkin pie consisted of putting cream, honey, spices, and eggs into the empty cavity of a pumpkin and baking it. Hollowed-out pumpkins could also be dried and used as storage containers, and dried strips of the skin could be pounded and woven into mats.

■ ■ ■ ■ ■ ■ ■ ■ ■ ■ ■

Poached Pears
with Cranberry Compote

Yields 8 servings

1½ cups orange juice or water

¾ cup light brown
   sugar, packed

¾ teaspoon cinnamon

4 large, firm pears (innkeeper's
   preference: Bartlett), peeled and
   halved, seeds removed

¾ cup cranberries, fresh or frozen

Vanilla yogurt, for garnish
   (optional)

1. Combine the orange juice, sugar, and cinnamon in a saucepan. Bring to a boil over medium heat, stirring until the sugar dissolves.

2. Add the pears and cranberries. Reduce the heat, then cover and simmer, stirring occasionally, for 10 minutes, or until the pears are tender (depending on the type of pear you use, this could take up to 20 minutes).

3. Using a slotted spoon, remove the pears from the compote and place them on individual serving dishes. Pour the reserved cranberry compote onto and around the sides of each pear.

4. Serve warm, topped with a dollop of vanilla yogurt, if desired.

TOPIA INN

An "oasis of organic luxury" is Topia Inn's signature description. Its rooms feature organic bedding and bath and body-care products. The innkeepers are committed to green living and have worked to create spaces that are in harmony with the natural beauty of the northern Berkshires. If guests care to pull themselves away from the steam and rain showers, chromatherapy, massages, and other body therapies offered at the inn, there are many opportunities to experience the outdoors and the arts, with Jacob's Pillow Dance Festival and several theater groups nearby.

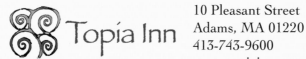

10 Pleasant Street
Adams, MA 01220
413-743-9600
www.topiainn.com

Baked Tortilla

This recipe is the inn's variation on the Spanish *tortilla de patata*,
or "potato omelet." Although the original is usually cooked on the stovetop
and then baked, this version is steam-baked.

Chilled Cantaloupe Soup

Cantaloupe soup is simple to make and so refreshing
on a hot summer morning.

Poached Pears with Raspberry Sauce

You can use cherry jam or conserve in place of raspberry, depending on the
season and your preference. You can also vary the berries for the garnish;
whatever is in season and fresh is the best.

Baked Tortilla

Yields 9 servings

2 tablespoons rosemary-infused
organic coconut oil (box,
below), plus more for greasing
the pan and brushing on the
finished tortilla

6 medium organic potatoes, peeled

2 large organic yams or
sweet potatoes

2 medium organic onions,
diced fine

1 teaspoon sea salt

1 tablespoon organic dried lemon
thyme

1 tablespoon organic dried
rosemary (save a little to
sprinkle on top)

8 organic jumbo eggs, beaten

Making Infused Coconut Oils

Bruise about 2 tablespoons of rosemary
leaves (or other herbs of your choice)
by rubbing them between two fingers.
This will help release their flavor
and aroma. Place the rosemary in a
decorative bottle with a stopper. Warm
enough coconut oil to fill the bottle to
a temperature of 140°F. Fill the bottle
and cap it. Let it sit for 2 weeks at
room temperature before using.

1. Preheat the oven to 350°F.

2. Grease a 9 x 9-inch steam-oven baking pan
   with rosemary-infused coconut oil.

3. Slice the potatoes and yams to ¼-inch thickness
   and set aside.

4. Toss the onions with the salt, 2 tablespoons of
   rosemary-infused coconut oil, lemon thyme,
   and rosemary until the onions are well coated.

5. Place a layer of potatoes in overlapping rows on
   the bottom of the baking pan.

6. Spread half of the onions over the first layer of
   potatoes.

7. Add a layer of yams in overlapping rows over
   the layer of onions.

8. Spread the remaining onions over the layer
   of yams.

9. Finish with another layer of potatoes and
   sprinkle rosemary over the top.

10. Steam-bake for 20 minutes (25 minutes in
    a convection oven), or until slightly brown
    on top.

11. Pour the eggs into the pan over the potato
    layers and bake for another 20 minutes.

12. Cut the tortilla into squares. Brush with
    rosemary-infused coconut oil before serving.

Chilled Cantaloupe Soup

Yields 4 servings

1 large organic cantaloupe

1 cup organic apricot nectar

Organic mint leaves and fresh berries, for garnish

1. Cut the cantaloupe in half and remove the seeds. Slice the fruit away from the peel.

2. Put the cantaloupe in a blender and purée.

3. Add the apricot nectar and blend until completely incorporated.

4. Pour the soup into a container, cover, and chill in the refrigerator for at least 1 hour.

5. To serve, ladle the soup into bowls and garnish with a mint leaf and some seasonal berries.

Poached Pears with Raspberry Sauce

Yields 2 servings

2 local ripe organic pears (any variety)

2 tablespoons organic raspberry jam or conserve, preferably homemade

Fresh organic raspberries, blackberries, and mint leaves, for garnish

1. Peel the pears and cut them in half, leaving the stem in place. Core the center of each half.

2. It is best if the pears are steam-baked in a steam oven for about 20 minutes. If you don't have a steam oven, you can put a small amount of water in the bottom of a pan, bring to a simmer over low heat, and steam the pears, cut-side down, for about 20 minutes, or until soft enough to cut with a spoon.

3. Heat the raspberry jam in a small pan over low heat for about 2 minutes, or until just melted and syrupy.

4. Place 2 pear halves side by side, cut-side up, in each of two bowls. Pour the heated jam sauce over the top. Garnish with fresh berries and a mint leaf and serve.

WHITE SWAN
BED AND BREAKFAST

The White Swan occupies a historic farmhouse built in 1820 and located in an area steeped in early Colonial history. This family-friendly B&B is minutes from Plimoth Plantation, Plymouth Rock, and the *Mayflower II*. A beautiful beach is just a short walk away.

146 Manomet Point Road
Plymouth, MA 02360
508-224-3759
www.whiteswan.com

Caramelized Baked French Toast

Top off this tasty French toast with fresh fruit in season. Across the street from the White Swan is Holmes Farm, which keeps the inn supplied with strawberries, blueberries, and other fresh fruits during the warm-weather months.

Cranberry-Zucchini Bread

This robust quick bread is made with cranberries from the bogs in Plymouth and native zucchini from the White Swan's garden.

Local Color

First Stop: Plymouth? Locals claim that, although not as well known, Manomet Point is where the *Mayflower* first stopped before the pilgrims settled in Plymouth.

Caramelized Baked French Toast

Yields 8 to 12 servings

½ cup (1 stick) salted butter

1 cup dark brown sugar, packed

6 large eggs

2 cups whole milk

½ cup cream or half-and-half

1 teaspoon vanilla extract

½ cup granulated sugar or sugar substitute

2 loaves cinnamon-raisin bread or any other bread of your choice (about 20 slices, cut in half)

Fresh fruit and whipped cream or yogurt (optional), for garnish

Warm maple syrup, for serving

1. Slowly melt the butter and brown sugar in a medium saucepan over low heat.

2. Coat a 12 x 9-inch ceramic pan with vegetable cooking spray and pour in the butter and brown sugar.

3. Whisk together the eggs, milk, cream, vanilla, and sugar.

4. Fit the bread slices into a single layer in the pan with the butter and brown sugar.

5. Pour the egg mixture over the bread. Cover and refrigerate overnight or long enough for the milk to soak into all of the bread.

6. When ready, preheat the oven to 350°F.

7. Bake for 45 minutes, or until brown on top.

8. To serve, top with fresh fruit and a dollop of whipped cream or yogurt, if desired. Serve with warm maple syrup.

Things to Do

Have a Historic Encounter

If you want to learn about all things Pilgrim and the experience of the early settlers in the New World, Plymouth is the right place to be. Within close proximity to the White Swan are Plymouth Rock, where the Pilgrims came ashore; Plimoth Plantation, a living history museum that demonstrates the life of the early colonists and Native Americans; the *Mayflower II*, a replica of the Pilgrims' ship; and many other related sites. To get an overview, visit the Plymouth visitors' center online (www.seeplymouth.com) or in person to plan your excursions.

Cranberry-Zucchini Bread

Yields 8 to 12 servings

1 cup cranberries

½ cup grated zucchini

1 cup cake flour

1 teaspoon baking powder

1 teaspoon baking soda

1 teaspoon salt

1 cup light brown sugar, packed

½ to 1 cup whole milk, as needed
    to moisten the dough

1. Preheat the oven to 350°F. Coat a 12 x 9-inch ceramic pan or a 9 x 5-inch loaf pan with vegetable cooking spray.

2. Steam the cranberries and zucchini in a microwave with ¼ cup of water for about 1½ minutes. Drain and let cool.

3. Place the flour, baking powder, baking soda, salt, and brown sugar in a large bowl and mix thoroughly.

4. Add the steamed cranberries and zucchini and enough milk to just moisten all the dry ingredients and make a thick dough.

5. Spoon the dough into the prepared pan and bake for 35 to 45 minutes, or until brown on top and a pick inserted in the center comes out clean.

Bear
Mountain
Lodge

Lovetts Inn

Inn at
Ellis
River

Hanover Inn

Squam
Lake Inn

The
Wakefield
Inn

The Lake House
at Ferry Point

Martin
Hill Inn

Inn by the Bandstand

New Hampshire

Live Free or Die

—State Motto

BEAR MOUNTAIN LODGE

Set in the heart of the White Mountains, Bear Mountain Lodge is designed for couples who are looking for a romantic escape. Guests relax in rustic luxury, with many of the rooms offering Jacuzzi tubs, steam showers, and fireplaces. Outdoors, the wraparound deck affords views of Mount Washington, and the outdoor hot tub is the perfect place to soak after a day of hiking at nearby Franconia Notch or Crawford Notch State Park.

3249 Main Street
Bethlehem NH 03574
603-869-2189
www.bearmountainlodge.net

Maple Sugar Waffles with Candied Pecans

Maple sugar is what's left after the sap of the sugar maple tree
is completely boiled away. You can use homemade or
purchased maple sugar to make this recipe.

Local Color

The nearby Mount Washington Cog Railway, built in 1869, was the
world's first mountain-climbing cog railway. Today, visitors can ride to
the top of the highest peak in the Northeast on a train powered by a
vintage steam locomotive or a more modern biodiesel engine.

Maple Sugar Waffles with Candied Pecans

Yields 5 to 6 large round waffles

Batter:

1¾ cups all-purpose flour

1 teaspoon salt

¼ cup granulated maple
sugar

1 tablespoon baking powder

1 teaspoon cinnamon

1 pinch grated nutmeg

1¼ cups 1% milk

½ cup pure maple syrup

4 large eggs, separated

½ cup (1 stick) unsalted
butter, melted and cooled

Candied pecans:

2 tablespoons unsalted
butter

2 tablespoons light brown
sugar, packed

¼ cup pure maple syrup

¾ cup coarsely chopped
pecans

Garnish:

Whipped cream and
sliced fruit

1. Combine the flour, salt, maple sugar, baking powder, cinnamon, and nutmeg in a large mixing bowl.

2. In a separate bowl, whisk together the milk, maple syrup, and egg yolks.

3. Mix the wet ingredients into the flour mixture. Do not overmix, but make sure all the flour is incorporated into the batter. There should be no flour left in the bottom of the bowl.

4. Stir in the butter.

5. Whip the egg whites with an electric mixer until stiff peaks form. Then fold the whites into the batter by hand. Again, do not overmix or you'll get tough waffles. Let the batter sit for about 10 minutes before using.

6. Cook the waffles in a Belgian waffle maker according to manufacturer's directions.

7. While the waffles cook, melt the butter for the pecans in a small frying pan over medium-low heat.

8. Stir in the brown sugar, maple syrup, and pecans. Cook for a few minutes until the pecans are nicely coated and the syrup thickens slightly.

9. To serve, either spoon the hot candied-pecan mixture over the waffles or let the mixture cool and sprinkle the sugary glazed pecans over the waffles. Garnish with whipped cream and sliced fruit.

Things to Do

Trek Mount Washington

Whether on foot or by car, a visit to the White Mountains would be incomplete without exploring this most famous landmark. Before you set out, here are some facts about this natural attraction:

- At 6,288 feet above sea level, Mount Washington is the highest peak east of the Mississippi River.

- Winds exceeding hurricane force occur there an average of 110 days a year.

- Mount Washington holds the record in the Northern and Western Hemispheres for directly measured surface wind speed: 231 miles per hour, recorded on the afternoon of April 12, 1934.

- Mount Washington's official record low temperature of –50°F was recorded on January 22, 1885. However, there is handwritten evidence to suggest that an unofficial low of –59°F occurred on January 5, 1871.

- Each year, more than 45,000 vehicles drive the Auto Road to the top of Mount Washington.

- The 8½-mile-long Crawford Path, which runs the length of the White Mountains' Presidential Range from Crawford Notch to Mount Washington's summit, is the oldest continuously maintained foot trail in the United States. It was originally built to the top of Mount Clinton by Abel Crawford and his son Ethan Allen Crawford in 1819. The Crawfords improved the trail as a bridle path, and in 1840, Abel, then seventy-five years old, made the first horseback ascent of Mount Washington. In 1870, the Crawford Path reverted back to a foot trail, and today, it is one of the most popular trails in the White Mountains.

- On the clearest days, observers at the summit of Mount Washington can see as far as New York's Mount Marcy, 134 miles to the west.

- It takes the average person almost 6½ hours to complete the 8½-mile round trip on the Tuckerman Ravine Trail, which begins on the southeastern side of Mount Washington.

INN AT ELLIS RIVER

Originally built as a farmhouse in 1893, the Inn at Ellis River also has a classic red barn and an icehouse that date from the same period. Perfect for lovers of natural beauty, the scenic White Mountain Forest surrounds Jackson on three sides, and there are plenty of opportunities to enjoy the great outdoors, including hiking, biking, fishing, canoeing, skiing, and snowshoeing. The area also offers many fun seasonal activities, such as the Haunted Hikes in October and an annual snow sculpture competition in winter.

17 Harriman Road
Jackson, NH 03846
603-383-9339
www.innatellisriver.com

House Specialties

Lemon Basil Coffee Cake

This delicious coffee cake was featured on a recent Inn-to-Inn Herb Tour. Raspberries can be substituted for the lemon basil to create another summer treat.

Frosty Virgin Mary

A refreshing version of a classic brunch cocktail, this drink features chives and fresh tomatoes. For a Frosty Bloody Mary, add 6 ounces of pepper or citrus vodka. If using pepper vodka, do not add ground pepper to the tomato mixture.

Maple-Banana-Bacon Muffins

Every March, the Inn at Ellis River celebrates maple sugaring season with special maple recipes. What better combination could there be than maple syrup and bacon for starting a chilly spring morning— or any morning, for that matter?

Chive and Cheddar Strata

Making a strata is a wonderful way to use any leftover bread from your local artisan bakery. For a heartier dish, add a cup of diced cooked ham, crumbled bacon, or sun-dried tomatoes when you add the cheese to the strata.

Local Color

An added attraction for gourmet travelers: The Inn at Ellis River participates in several Washington Valley themed "Inn to Inn" events, where chefs at area inns cook dishes appropriate to the theme. Guests are welcome to travel from inn to inn and sample the goodies. Past tours have included such themes as chocolate, herbs, maple syrup, Christmas cookies, and Halloween treats. To find the latest schedule of tours, go to www.mtwashingtonvalley.org and check Inn to Inn Tours under the Vacation Specials heading.

Lemon Basil Coffee Cake

Yields 15 slices

1 cup (2 sticks) unsalted
  butter, softened

2 cups granulated sugar

4 large eggs

½ teaspoon salt

3 cups all-purpose flour

1 tablespoon baking powder

1 cup whole milk

1½ teaspoons lemon oil
  (innkeeper's preference:
  Boyajian) or
  1 tablespoon lemon zest

2 tablespoons lemon basil
  leaves, chopped fine

Sprigs of lemon basil and
  lemon wheels, for garnish
  (optional)

1. Preheat the oven to 350°F. Grease a 10-cup Bundt pan.

2. Use an electric mixer to cream the butter and sugar until light and fluffy.

3. Add the eggs, one at a time, mixing until blended.

4. In a separate bowl, stir together the salt, flour, and baking powder.

5. Mix the flour mixture, alternating with milk, into the butter mixture, beginning and ending with flour.

6. Add the lemon oil and lemon basil and beat for 2 minutes. Do not overbeat.

7. Pour the batter into the Bundt pan and bake for about 45 minutes, or until a cake tester inserted in the center comes out clean.

8. Cool for 5 minutes, then remove the cake from the pan by inverting it onto a cooling rack and let it cool completely.

9. Cut into slices and garnish with lemon basil and lemon wheels, if desired.

Frosty Virgin Mary

Yields 4 servings

1½ cups grape tomatoes

1½ cups tomato juice, divided

2 green onions, chopped fine

¼ cup finely chopped chives

3 tablespoons freshly squeezed lemon juice

4 teaspoons Worcestershire sauce

½ teaspoon horseradish, or more to taste

6 dashes green Tabasco sauce, or more to taste

½ teaspoon sea salt

Freshly ground pepper

Chopped chives and lemon wheels, for garnish

1. Freeze the grape tomatoes.

2. To prepare the drinks, place the frozen tomatoes, half the tomato juice, the green onions, chives, lemon juice, Worcestershire, horseradish, Tabasco, and sea salt in a blender. Blend until all the ingredients are smooth and frosty.

3. Add the remaining tomato juice, season with pepper, and blend again.

4. Pour into glasses and garnish each with chopped chives and a lemon wheel. Serve immediately.

Maple-Banana-Bacon Muffins

Yields about 18 muffins

8 to 10 strips thick-sliced bacon

2 tablespoons light brown sugar

4 bananas

1 tablespoon baking powder

¼ teaspoon salt

3 cups all-purpose flour

1 large egg

1 cup whole milk

2 tablespoons canola oil

⅓ cup plus 3 tablespoons dark amber maple syrup, divided

4 teaspoons natural maple extract (innkeepers preference: Boyajian), divided

½ cup confectioners' sugar

½ tablespoon cream or whole milk

1. Preheat the oven to 400°F. Coat muffin tins with nonstick cooking spray.

2. Prepare the bacon by placing it on a parchment-lined baking sheet, rubbing it with brown sugar, and baking it in the oven until crisp, about 12 to 15 minutes. When cool, use scissors or a knife to cut it into small pieces. You should have about 1 cup of bacon pieces.

3. Turn the oven down to 350°F.

4. Mash three of the bananas and dice the fourth one, so that some small pieces of banana will be incorporated in the muffins.

5. Combine the baking powder, salt, and flour in a large bowl and form a well in the center of the mixture.

6. In a separate bowl, combine the egg, milk, oil, ⅓ cup of maple syrup, and 3 teaspoons of natural maple extract.

7. Add the mashed bananas to the egg mixture and pour into the well of the flour mixture.

8. Stir until just combined (you may need to use slightly more or less milk, depending on the ripeness of the bananas), then fold in the diced banana and ⅔ cup of the diced bacon.

9. Fill the muffin cups two-thirds full, and sprinkle the remaining ⅓ cup of diced bacon over the top of the muffins, reserving a little to sprinkle on after baking.

10. Bake for about 20 to 25 minutes, or until a toothpick inserted in the center comes out clean.

11. While the muffins cool on a wire rack, prepare a maple glaze by combining the 3 tablespoons of maple syrup, confectioners' sugar, cream, and remaining 1 teaspoon of maple extract. Add more sugar or liquid if needed to achieve the consistency required for drizzling.

12. Remove the muffins from the tin. Drizzle the glaze over the muffins and sprinkle with the reserved bacon pieces.

Chive and Cheddar Strata

Yields 8 to 12 servings

Note advance prep time.

½ loaf English toasting or other
firm textured bread, cubed (leave
crusts on)

2 cups shredded sharp cheddar cheese

¼ cup chopped chives

15 large eggs

1 tablespoon Dijon mustard

5 cups half-and-half

Sea salt and freshly ground pepper

Whole chives, for garnish

1 recipe Red Pepper and Tomato
Coulis (below), for serving

1. Butter a 13 x 9-inch baking pan.

2. Line the pan with half the bread cubes and cover
with half the cheese and chives. Use the remaining
bread to make another layer and cover with the
remaining cheese and chives.

3. Whisk together the eggs, mustard, half-and-half,
and salt and pepper to taste. Pour the egg mixture
over the top of the strata and refrigerate overnight.

4. In the morning, preheat the oven to 350°F.

5. Bake the strata until golden brown and puffed up,
about 1 hour. Let sit for 10 minutes to set before
slicing. Garnish with chives and serve with the
warm coulis.

Red Pepper and Tomato Coulis

1 tablespoon olive oil

1 large red bell pepper, diced

½ sweet onion (such as Vidalia or
Texas 1015), diced

5 to 6 garlic cloves, roasted

1 cup grape tomatoes

1 jar (8 ounces) sun-dried tomatoes
packed in oil

Salt and pepper

1. In a small skillet, heat the olive oil over low heat.
Sauté the pepper and onion until soft, about 5 to
7 minutes.

2. Place in a food processor and add the garlic,
grape tomatoes, and sun-dried tomatoes.

3. Process until smooth, adding more tomatoes if
needed to obtain desired consistency.

4. Season with salt and pepper to taste.

INN BY THE BANDSTAND

Built in 1809 for George Sullivan, a lawyer who was twice the State Attorney General for New Hampshire, this Federal-style townhouse has many of its original features. Wide-plank wood floors and high ceilings with crown moldings grace many of the rooms. The inn also has eleven working fireplaces. The bandstand across the street from the inn was given to the town in 1916 by resident Ambrose Swasey to beautify the square.

6 Front Street
Exeter, NH 03833
603-772-6352
www.innbythebandstand.com

House Specialties

Summer Corn Fritters

At the inn, these fritters are served with New Hampshire maple syrup and bacon.

Blueberry Crumb Cake

This is a delicious breakfast treat, especially in the summer
when blueberries are at their peak.

Local Color

A short walk from the Inn by the Bandstand is the American
Independence Museum, which was the site of the New Hampshire
Treasury during the American Revolution. It contains early drafts
of the United States Constitution and offers self-guided tours and
historical information about the area and its importance
in our nation's founding history.

Summer Corn Fritters

Yields 4 to 6 servings

1 cup corn kernels, cut from 1 to 2 ears

1 large egg, separated

2 teaspoons all-purpose flour

½ teaspoon baking powder

½ teaspoon salt

Paprika, to taste

Vegetable oil, for frying

Chopped fresh parsley, for garnish (optional)

1. Shuck the corn and boil in salted water for 20 minutes. Drain and remove the corn kernels from the cobs and place them in a medium bowl.

2. Beat the egg yolk until thickened and fold into the corn kernels.

3. In another bowl, sift together the flour, baking powder, salt, and paprika.

4. Add the flour mixture to the corn kernels and stir gently until they're covered in flour.

5. Beat the egg white until stiff and fold into the corn mixture.

6. Pour enough oil into a large nonstick pan to just cover the bottom and heat to 370°F (use a candy thermometer to measure).

7. Drop the corn mixture by the tablespoon into the oil. Cook until delicately browned on both sides, about 2 minutes per side.

8. Drain the fritters on paper towels, garnish with parsley, if desired, and serve immediately.

Blueberry Crumb Cake

Yields 18 slices

½ cup (1 stick) unsalted butter, chilled and cut into ¼-inch bits, plus ½ cup (1 stick), softened

3¼ cups all-purpose flour, divided

2 cups granulated sugar, divided

1 teaspoon cinnamon

1 tablespoon baking powder

½ teaspoon nutmeg

¼ teaspoon ground cloves

1 teaspoon salt

3 large eggs

¾ cup 2% milk

3 cups fresh blueberries, washed, stems removed, and dried on paper towels

2 cups heavy cream, whipped, for serving

1. Preheat the oven to 375°F. Grease and flour a 13 x 9-inch baking dish.

2. Prepare the crumb topping: Mix the chilled butter with ¾ cup of flour, 1 cup of sugar, and the cinnamon in a medium bowl.

3. Rub the butter into the other ingredients with your fingers until the mixture resembles coarse meal or sand. Set aside.

4. Sift together the remaining flour, baking powder, nutmeg, cloves, and salt in a medium bowl.

5. In a mixing bowl, with an electric mixer, cream together the softened butter and the remaining sugar.

6. Beat in the eggs, one at a time.

7. Add the flour mixture in thirds, alternating with the milk, and beat well after each addition.

8. Gently fold in the blueberries.

9. Pour the batter into the prepared baking dish and sprinkle the crumb topping evenly over the top.

10. Bake for 40 to 50 minutes, or until the top is golden and a toothpick inserted in the center of the cake comes out clean.

11. Serve warm or at room temperature, topped with a dollop of whipped cream.

LOVETTS INN

Lovetts started out as a private estate known as the Lafayette Brook Farm. In 1928, it was transformed into a New England country inn and renamed Lovetts Inn. Over the years, the inn has hosted several celebrities, including many of the Kennedys and Hollywood legend Bette Davis. Hiking, skiing, and viewing the fall foliage are among the activities that guests enjoy during their stay at Lovetts.

1474 Profile Road
Franconia, NH 03580
603-823-7761
www.lovettsinn.com

House Specialties

Apple-Cranberry Muffins

Apples and cranberries are a perfect fall combination.

Whole-Grain Pancakes

If you like, you can add fruit or nuts to these pancakes
on the griddle before you flip them.

Cranberry-Dried Apricot Cream Scones

These scones are a sweet breakfast treat and are equally nice for afternoon tea.

Apple-Cranberry Muffins

Yields 12 muffins

½ cup (1 stick) salted butter, at room temperature

¾ cup granulated sugar

2 medium eggs

2 cups all-purpose flour

½ teaspoon salt

¼ teaspoon cinnamon

2 teaspoons baking powder

½ cup whole milk

1 teaspoon vanilla extract

1 cup cranberries, fresh or frozen

1½ cups Granny Smith apples, peeled and chopped

1. Preheat the oven to 375°F. Grease a 12-cup muffin tin.

2. Using an electric mixer set on low speed, cream the butter and sugar. Add the eggs, one at a time, beating after each.

3. In a separate bowl, sift together the flour, salt, cinnamon, and baking powder.

4. Add to the butter mixture. Then add the milk and vanilla and mix well.

5. Fold in the cranberries and apples by hand.

6. Bake for 30 minutes, or until golden brown.

Whole-Grain Pancakes

Yields 4 to 6 servings

1 cup buckwheat or oatmeal flour (or a combination of the two)

3 teaspoons baking powder

¼ cup whole wheat flour

¾ teaspoon salt

1¾ cups whole milk

2 tablespoons salted butter, melted

2 medium eggs, well beaten

1. Combine all the ingredients and beat well.

2. Lightly butter a griddle heated to 300°F and spoon on the batter.

3. Cook the pancakes for 1 to 2 minutes, or until bubbly and the underside is brown. Flip over and cook for 1 minute more, or until cooked through.

Cranberry-Dried Apricot Cream Scones

Yields 8 to 10 scones

2 cups all-purpose flour

1 tablespoon baking powder

½ teaspoon salt

¼ cup granulated sugar,
plus 2 tablespoons
for sprinkling

⅓ cup dried cranberries

⅓ cup dried apricots,
chopped

1¼ cups heavy cream

3 tablespoons salted
butter, melted

1. Preheat the oven to 425°F. Grease a 10-inch springform pan.

2. Combine the flour, baking powder, and salt in a bowl with ¼ cup of sugar, mixing well.

3. Add the dried cranberries and apricots.

4. With a fork, stir in the cream until the dough holds together.

5. Knead the dough on a lightly floured board for 2 to 3 minutes and pat into a 10-inch circle. Spread the melted butter on the top and sides and sprinkle with 2 tablespoons of sugar.

6. Place the dough in the prepared pan and bake for about 25 minutes, or until lightly browned.

7. Cool 3 or 4 minutes on a cooling rack. Slice into wedges and serve.

Things to Do

Celebrate Lupines

If you happen to be in New Hampshire during the month of June, you'll be treated to a beautiful sight: The fields and pastures of the entire White Mountain region are carpeted with vibrant purple, pink, blue, and white lupines. The area pays homage to these spiky flowers with an annual Celebration of Lupines. Greenhouses and garden centers sell Lupine seeds and plants, and Franconia and neighboring towns offer a month of special events. See www.franconianotch.org/things-to-do/special-events/ for more information on the festival.

MARTIN HILL INN

Housed in two early nineteenth-century homes, Martin Hill Inn is a gardener's delight. More than twenty-five varieties of perennials grace its gardens. Strategically placed seating areas give guests places to relax and enjoy the grounds and, perhaps, sip a glass of wine or lemonade. Portsmouth's Market Square and other area attractions, including historic sites, museums, and theaters as well as restaurants and shops, are just a short walk away.

404 Islington Street
Portsmouth, NH 03801
603-436-2287
www.martinhillinn.com

House Specialties

Teacup Pumpkin Mousse

Serving this mousse in teacups makes for a beautiful presentation and a great way to show off a collection.

Tomato-Pesto Strata

This dish makes great use of an abundant tomato crop.

Local Color

Portsmouth was named one of the top 100 walking cities in America by *Prevention* magazine. Visitors to this seaside town can find buildings from the 1800s cozying up to more modern structures. A rich mix of sidewalk cafes, shops, galleries, and restaurants makes for a very enjoyable afternoon.

Teacup Pumpkin Mousse

Yields 6 to 8 servings, depending on teacup size

2 cups whole milk

1 box (4 ounces) vanilla or butterscotch cook-and-serve pudding

¼ cup cranberry juice

1 envelope (1 ounce) unflavored gelatin

3 tablespoons light brown sugar

1 teaspoon nutmeg

1½ teaspoons cinnamon

1 cup pumpkin purée

1 cup heavy cream

3 tablespoons confectioners' sugar

1 teaspoon vanilla bean paste

Whipped cream and 2 to 3 crushed ginger snaps, for garnish

1. Add the milk to the pudding in a medium saucepan. Cook on medium heat, whisking constantly until the pudding starts to thicken, about 5 minutes.

2. Pour the cranberry juice into a large bowl and sprinkle on the gelatin. Stir to combine.

3. Add the pudding mix to the gelatin mix, whisking to combine. Set aside.

4. In a separate medium bowl, mix the brown sugar, nutmeg, and cinnamon into the pumpkin purée, then add to the pudding mix. If the mixture is still warm, allow it to cool to room temperature.

5. Put the heavy cream, confectioners' sugar, and vanilla bean paste into the bowl of an electric mixer and use the whisk attachment to beat until soft peaks form. Gently fold into the pudding mix until incorporated (some streaks are okay).

6. Fill the teacups with mousse and refrigerate, covered, until set, 1 to 2 hours or overnight.

7. Before serving, garnish the mousse with whipped cream and ginger snaps.

Tomato-Pesto Strata

Yields 6 to 8 servings

Note advance prep time.

6 to 8 cups bread cubes from
a loaf of sourdough bread
or ciabatta, toasted

1 cup pesto

12 ounces fresh baby spinach

4 ripe tomatoes (preferably heirloom)

1 pint bocconcini (small, fresh
mozzarella balls), cut in half

8 slices prosciutto, chopped coarse

8 large eggs

3 cups half-and-half

Salt and pepper

Chopped basil and parsley leaves, fresh
fruit, and tomato slices, for garnish

1. Preheat the oven to 375°F. Lightly grease a
13 x 9-inch casserole.

2. Place half of the bread cubes into the casserole.
Layer half of the pesto, spinach, tomato,
bocconcini, and prosciutto over the bread cubes.
Add the rest of the bread cubes and layer the
remaining pesto, spinach, tomato, bocconcini, and
prosciutto over the top.

3. Whisk the eggs and half-and-half together in a
bowl. Season with salt and pepper.

4. Pour the egg mixture over the casserole. Cover
and refrigerate overnight.

5. Cook, covered, for 25 minutes, then uncover and
finish cooking for 20 minutes, or until set.

6. Let the strata set up for 10 minutes before cutting.
Sprinkle basil and parsley over the top and garnish
with fruit and tomato slices before serving.

THE LAKE HOUSE AT FERRY POINT

Listen for the loons at one of the few lakefront inns in New Hampshire's Lakes Region. The Lake House at Ferry Point offers spectacular views and easy access to Lake Winnisquam for swimming and boating. The inn is set in an area that abounds in natural beauty and outdoor activities. Franconia Notch State Park and White Mountain National Forest are close by.

100 Lower Bay Road
Sanbornton, NH 03269
603-524-0087
www.new-hampshire-inn.com

House Specialties

Wild Blueberry Strata

This wonderfully colorful egg dish can be enjoyed year-round since it works with both fresh and frozen wild blueberries.

New Hampshire Maple Whipped Cream

This whipped cream is great on berries, pies, baked fruit desserts— basically anything that you would put regular whipped cream on.

Wild Blueberry Strata

Yields 8 to 12 servings

Note advance prep time.

1 loaf cinnamon bread (about 20 slices), cubed (day-old bread works very well)

2 cups wild blueberries, fresh or frozen

6 large eggs

2½ cups whole milk

1 tablespoon cinnamon

1 teaspoon pure vanilla extract

1. Coat a 15 x 10-inch baking dish with vegetable cooking spray.

2. Cover the bottom of the dish with half of the bread cubes.

3. Layer the blueberries evenly on top of the bread.

4. Cover the blueberries with the remaining bread cubes.

5. In a mixing bowl, whisk together the eggs, milk, cinnamon, and vanilla.

6. Pour the egg mixture over the bread in the baking dish, making sure all the bread cubes are moist. Cover with aluminum foil and chill overnight in the refrigerator.

7. In the morning, preheat the oven to 350°F.

8. Bake the strata, covered, for 30 minutes. Remove the aluminum foil and bake for another 30 minutes, or until puffed and golden.

9. Cut into squares and serve hot.

New Hampshire Maple Whipped Cream

Yields 1½ to 2 cups

1 cup heavy whipping cream

3 tablespoons pure New Hampshire maple syrup (Grade B or Grade A)

¼ teaspoon pure vanilla extract

1. With an electric mixer or by hand, whisk together the cream, maple syrup, and vanilla until stiff peaks form. Use immediately. Store any unused portion in an airtight container for up to 10 hours. When ready to use, whisk again for 10 to 15 seconds.

Things to Do

Find a Lost River

If you tire of lake activities, consider exploring Lost River Gorge and Boulder Caves (www.findlostriver.com). Formed by glaciers millions of years ago, the gorge is named "Lost River" because a stream draining part of Kinsman Notch disappears below the surface for a stretch before emerging and joining the Pemigewasset River. Following along the stream, hikers can explore several caves that drop down from the rocky trail. For extra adventure, night tours through lantern-lit caves are also available.

THE WAKEFIELD INN

The Wakefield Inn is ideally situated for exploring the New Hampshire White Mountains or Lakes Region, as well as the seacoasts of both New Hampshire and Maine. Originally built in 1804, the inn has preserved many period details, such as a three-sided fireplace with a beehive oven, a wraparound front porch, and a stunning "flying" spiral staircase, which rises three floors with no center pole support.

2723 Wakefield Road
Wakefield, NH 03872
603-522-8272
www.wakefieldinn.com

Pumpkin Muffins
with Cream Cheese Filling

These rich and delicious muffins contain a sweet surprise.

Eggs Benedict Casserole

This breakfast classic has all the yummy flavors of the original but is a whole lot less hassle to prepare!

Tasty Tidbit

The first potato patch in the United States was planted in Londonderry, New Hampshire, in 1719.

Pumpkin Muffins with Cream Cheese Filling

Yields 12 muffins

Note advance prep time.

Cream cheese filling:

4 ounces cream cheese, at room temperature

½ cup confectioners' sugar

1½ teaspoons vanilla extract

Streusel topping:

½ cup all-purpose flour

⅓ cup granulated sugar

¼ cup pecans, chopped

½ teaspoon cinnamon

3 tablespoons unsalted butter, melted

Muffins:

1½ cups all-purpose flour

1 teaspoon cinnamon

1 teaspoon nutmeg

½ teaspoon ground cloves

½ teaspoon baking soda

½ teaspoon salt

2 medium eggs

1 cup granulated sugar

1 cup canned pumpkin purée

½ cup plus 2 tablespoons vegetable oil

½ teaspoon vanilla extract

1. Make the cream cheese filling: In a medium bowl, stir together the cream cheese and confectioners' sugar until smooth. Add the vanilla and stir to combine.

2. Form the mixture into a 12-inch log on a piece of plastic wrap. Wrap and freeze for at least 2 hours.

3. Preheat the oven to 350°F. Line a standard 12-cup muffin tin with paper liners and set aside.

4. Make the streusel topping: Use a fork to combine the flour, sugar, pecans, cinnamon, and butter in a medium bowl. Set aside.

5. Make the muffins: Whisk together the flour, cinnamon, nutmeg, cloves, baking soda, and salt in a large bowl.

6. In a medium bowl, whisk together the eggs, sugar, pumpkin, oil, and vanilla.

7. Pour the pumpkin mixture over the dry ingredients. Use a rubber spatula to gently combine the batter, mixing just until the dry ingredients are moistened.

8. Remove the cream cheese from the freezer and divide it into twelve 1-inch slices.

9. Scoop a small amount of batter into the muffin cups. Place 1 slice of the cream cheese log right in the center of each cup, then fill with the remaining batter.

10. Sprinkle the pecan streusel on top of each muffin. Press on the streusel lightly to make sure it adheres to the batter.

11. Bake until golden, about 20 to 25 minutes. Cool in the pan for about 5 minutes, then remove the muffins to a cooling rack to cool completely. Store in an airtight container in the refrigerator for up to 1 week. Let the muffins come to room temperature before serving.

Eggs Benedict Casserole

Yields 8 to 12 servings

Note advance prep time.

Casserole:

12 ounces Canadian bacon, coarsely chopped

6 English muffins, split and cut into 1-inch pieces

8 medium eggs

2 cups 2% milk

1 teaspoon onion powder

¼ teaspoon paprika

Hollandaise sauce:

4 egg yolks

½ cup heavy whipping cream

2 tablespoons lemon juice

1 teaspoon Dijon mustard

½ cup salted butter, melted

Garnish:

Chopped chives

1. Make the casserole: Place half of the Canadian bacon in a greased 13 x 9-inch baking dish. Top with the English muffins and remaining bacon.

2. In a large bowl, whisk the eggs, milk, and onion powder together and pour over top of the English muffins and bacon.

3. Refrigerate, covered, overnight.

4. In the morning, preheat the oven to 375°F.

5. Remove the casserole from the refrigerator while the oven heats. Sprinkle the top with paprika.

6. Bake, covered, for 35 minutes. Uncover and bake 10 to 15 minutes longer, or until a knife inserted near the center comes out clean.

7. Make the hollandaise sauce: In the top of a double boiler or a metal bowl over simmering water, whisk the egg yolks, cream, lemon juice, and mustard until blended.

8. Whisking constantly, cook until the mixture is just thick enough to coat a metal spoon and the temperature reaches 160°F, about 5 to 7 minutes.

9. Reduce the heat to very low. Very slowly drizzle in the warm melted butter, whisking constantly.

10. Garnish the casserole with chopped chives and serve with the hollandaise sauce.

HANOVER INN

Originally home to General Ebenezer Brewster, who became Dartmouth College Steward in 1769, the inn has evolved with the college. In 1780, Brewster turned his home into a tavern. In the early 1800s, Brewster's son had the tavern moved to another site and began building a much larger edifice that eventually, after several renovations and expansions, became the Hanover Inn. Today, the inn overlooks the beautiful Dartmouth campus and has the distinction of being the longest continuously operating inn in New Hampshire.

Two East Wheelock
Hanover, NH 03755
603-643-4300
www.hanoverinn.com

House Specialties

Duck and Green Chile Hash with Poached Eggs and Chipotle Hollandaise

The duck legs need time to cure, and the confit for this recipe has to bake for about 3 hours, so plan to start this dish the day before.

Homemade Sage and Ginger Breakfast Sausage

Although making the sausage takes a bit of work, you'll be able to enjoy the fruits of your labor for a while. Keep the sausage rolls in the freezer and slice and fry up patties as needed.

Duck and Green Chile Hash with Poached Eggs and Chipotle Hollandaise

Yields 4 servings

Note advance prep time.

2 cups small marble potatoes

1 teaspoon canola oil

1 medium poblano chile pepper

Salt and pepper

2 tablespoons extra-virgin olive oil

1 garlic clove, thinly sliced

1 small Spanish onion, julienned and caramelized

1 teaspoon red pepper flakes

4 duck legs, cooked, skin removed, and meat pulled from bone (Duck Confit, page 169)

2 teaspoons sherry vinegar

2 tablespoons distilled vinegar

8 large eggs

1 recipe Chipotle Hollandaise (page 170), for drizzling

Watercress, for garnish

1. Place the potatoes and 1 quart of water in a medium pot. Bring the water to a simmer and cook the potatoes until they are fork tender.

2. Remove the potatoes from the water and put them on a sheet pan in the refrigerator until cool, about 30 minutes. Then lightly press down on the potatoes to give them a "smashed" appearance.

3. Preheat the oven to 350°F. Place the canola oil, poblano chile pepper, and salt in a small, ovenproof dish and mix well to coat the pepper. Bake for 15 minutes. Remove from the oven, place in a small mixing bowl, and cover with plastic wrap. This will make it easier remove the outer skin of the pepper.

4. Once the pepper is cool enough to handle, remove the skin and seeds. Dice the pepper into small cubes.

5. Place the olive oil and garlic in a medium sauté pan and cook on medium heat until the garlic starts to brown on the edges. At this point, add the potatoes, onion, poblano pepper, red pepper flakes, and duck meat.

6. Finish the sauté with the sherry vinegar and season with salt and pepper.

7. In a medium pot, bring 2 quarts of water and the distilled vinegar to a simmer. Crack the eggs into a shallow dish and slide them into the simmering water. Cook until soft poached, about 2 to 3 minutes.

8. Divide the duck and green chile hash between 4 plates. Add the poached eggs and drizzle with chipotle hollandaise. Garnish with watercress.

Duck Confit

2 tablespoons salt

2 tablespoons light brown sugar

4 Long Island duck legs

4 sprigs thyme

10 peppercorns

1 bay leaf

3 cups rendered duck fat (duck fat can be purchased or canola oil may be substituted)

1. Put the salt and brown sugar into a bowl and mix well.

2. Rub the duck legs with the salt and sugar mixture and let cure in the refrigerator for up to 24 hours.

3. Once the duck legs have cured, rinse off the excess salt and sugar and pat dry with a paper towel.

4. Preheat the oven to 300°F.

5. Place the duck legs, thyme, peppercorns, and bay leaf in a 4-inch-deep baking dish and cover with duck fat. Cover with aluminum foil and bake for 3 hours, or until very tender. The duck meat should easily pull away from the bone.

6. Cool the legs in the duck fat and refrigerate until you are ready to use.

Chipotle Hollandaise

4 egg yolks

Salt and pepper

2 teaspoons lemon juice

1 teaspoon sherry
vinegar

2 teaspoons puréed
chipotles in
adobo sauce

12 ounces warm,
clarified unsalted
butter (purchased or
homemade)

1. Bring 2 cups of water to a gentle simmer in a medium saucepan or in the bottom of a double boiler. Do not let the water boil.

2. Place the egg yolks, salt and pepper, lemon juice, sherry vinegar, 1 teaspoon of water, and chipotles in a medium heatproof mixing bowl that will sit on the top of the saucepan without touching the water or in the top of the double boiler and whisk for 2 to 3 minutes until the mixture lightens in color.

3. Place the mixture over the simmering water and continue to whisk until it has thickened enough to coat the back of a spoon.

4. While whisking, slowly add the clarified butter to the egg mixture. Continue whisking until all the butter is incorporated and you have a stable hollandaise sauce.

5. Season with salt and pepper and reserve in a warm place until serving

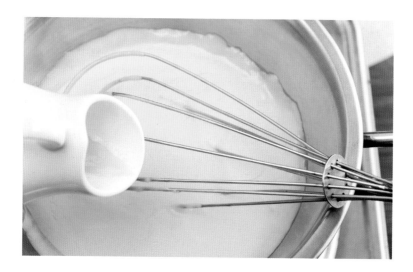

Homemade Sage and Ginger Breakfast Sausage

Yields about 45 sausage patties

5 pounds boneless
    pork butt, diced

⅓ cup sage leaves, tightly packed
    and finely chopped

3 garlic cloves, minced

½ cup peeled and finely
    minced ginger

3 teaspoons black pepper

3½ tablespoons kosher salt

2 tablespoons chopped thyme

½ cup Vermont maple syrup

1 cup ice water

Parsley and watercress,
    for garnish (optional)

1. Put 2 cups of ice and 1 cup of cold water in a large mixing bowl to create an ice bath. Place a medium mixing bowl on top of the ice bath to keep the sausage mixture chilled as you are making it.

2. Place all of the ingredients except the maple syrup and ice water in the medium bowl. Mix thoroughly, remove from the ice bath, and let rest for 30 minutes in the refrigerator.

3. While the mixture is resting, place all of the meat grinder attachments in the freezer for 20 minutes. This will help keep the sausage mixture cold while grinding.

4. Grind the sausage mixture using the large die. Change to the small die and run the mixture through the grinder a second time.

5. Place the ground mixture into a large electric mixer and add the maple syrup. Mix the sausage with the paddle attachment on medium speed and slowly add the ice water. Continue mixing for approximately 1 minute after all the water has been added.

6. Remove the sausage from the bowl, place it on a large piece of plastic wrap, and mold it into long tube shapes, approximately 1½ inches in diameter. Freeze the sausage tubes and slice them into 2-ounce patties when ready to cook.

7. In a medium sauté pan or on a griddle, cook the breakfast sausage until crispy on the outside. The internal temperature of the sausage should be 150°F when cooked.

8. Garnish with parsley and watercress, if desired.

SQUAM LAKE INN

Originally a farmhouse built in 1895, Squam Lake Inn is furnished in comfortable New England style. It's a short walk or drive away from Squam Lake, where the 1981 movie *On Golden Pond* was filmed. Guests can take a boat tour of the lake, explore the nearby White Mountains, or hike Lafayette Mountain at Franconia Notch State Park.

28 Shepard Hill Road
Holderness, NH 03245
603-968-4417
www.squamlakeinn.com

Orange-Cream French Toast

Every slice of this delectable French toast contains a sweet, rich filling.

Four-Grain Blueberry Pancakes

These pancakes combine the goodness of four grains
with the great taste of fresh blueberries.

Sweet Additions

For a nice variation in the fall, use julienned apples sprinkled
lightly with cinnamon and sugar in place of the blueberries in
the pancakes. You can also make them without any fruit at all if
you have some "plain" eaters at your table.

Orange-Cream French Toast

Yields 6 to 8 servings

4 ounces cream cheese, at room
    temperature

1 tablespoon orange juice

2 tablespoons granulated sugar,
    divided

1 teaspoon orange zest

1 large loaf French bread, unsliced

4 large eggs

1 cup whole milk

1 teaspoon vanilla extract

Orange marmalade,
    for topping (optional)

1. In a small bowl, mix together the cream cheese, orange juice, 1 tablespoon of sugar, and orange zest until blended.

2. Slice the end off the bread and discard. Cut the next slice ½ inch thick and only three-fourths of the way through the loaf to form a pocket. Cut the next ½-inch-thick slice all the way through. Continue to do this until all the bread is sliced. (You'll have 9 or 10 slices, each with a pocket.)

3. Spread about 1 tablespoon of cream cheese filling in each pocket, then press the pockets together.

4. In a large, shallow bowl, whisk together the eggs, milk, 1 tablespoon of sugar, and vanilla.

5. Dip each slice of stuffed bread in the batter, turning to coat, and place on a plate or shallow pan until all the slices are coated.

6. Preheat a large nonstick skillet or griddle over medium heat. Add a little butter and swirl to coat the skillet. When the butter foams, place the soaked bread pockets in the pan and cook until lightly browned, about 3 minutes on each side, turning once.

7. Remove from the skillet, top with orange marmalade, if desired, and serve immediately.

Four-Grain Blueberry Pancakes

Yields 4 to 6 servings

1½ cups all-purpose flour

2 heaping tablespoons
 old-fashioned oats

2 heaping tablespoons wheat germ

2 tablespoons yellow cornmeal

¾ teaspoon baking soda

1½ teaspoons baking powder

2 teaspoons granulated sugar

¼ teaspoon salt

2 large eggs, beaten

1½ cups buttermilk

¼ cup whole milk

4 tablespoons unsalted butter, melted

1 pint fresh blueberries, washed

1. Mix the flour, oats, wheat germ, cornmeal, baking soda, baking powder, sugar, and salt together in a small bowl.

2. In a large bowl, combine the eggs, buttermilk, and whole milk, using a fork.

3. Mix in the dry ingredients just until blended. Do not overmix.

4. Stir the melted butter into the batter.

5. Preheat a griddle or large skillet to medium high. Generously grease with butter.

6. Pour about ¼ cup of batter per pancake onto the griddle and dot with blueberries.

7. Cook until bubbles appear in the center of the pancake. Flip and finish cooking until golden brown, another 1 or 2 minutes.

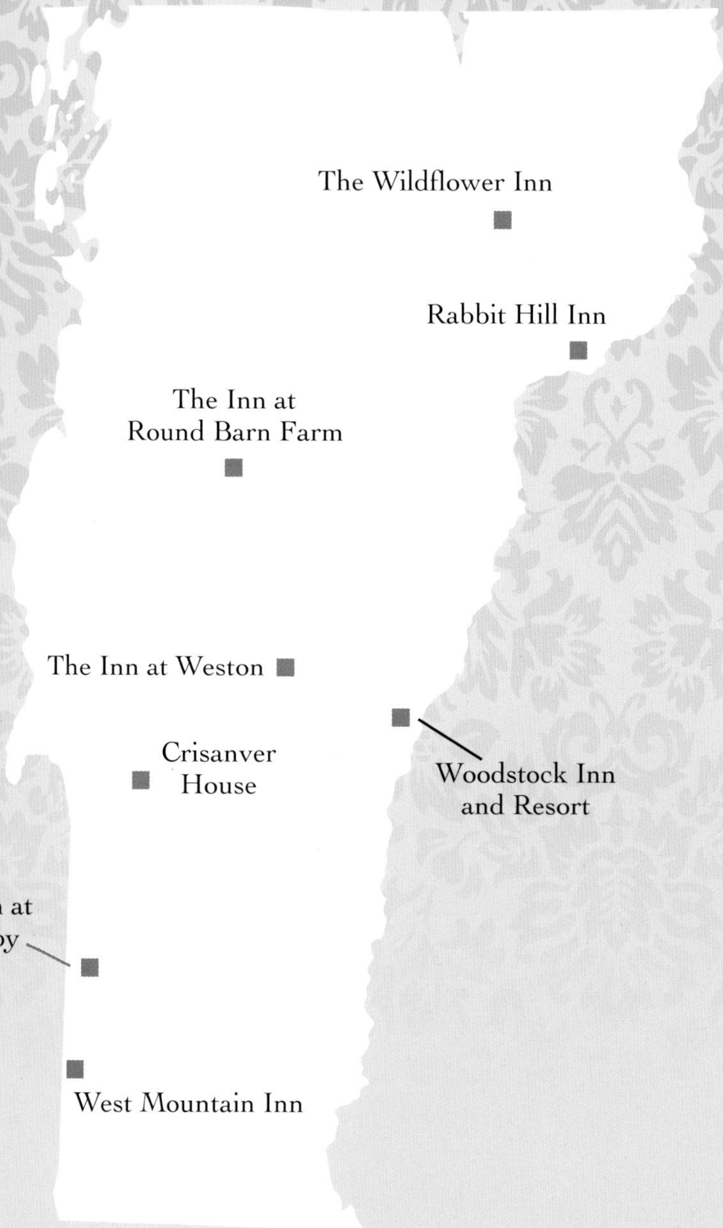

The Wildflower Inn

Rabbit Hill Inn

The Inn at
Round Barn Farm

The Inn at Weston

Crisanver
House

Woodstock Inn
and Resort

The Inn at
Ormsby
Hill

West Mountain Inn

Vermont

In my travels, I am reminded that the wellspring of Vermont liberty flows from Main Street, not State Street; from town meeting democracy, not government bureaucracy; and from the home of every Vermonter.

—James H. Douglas, Jr.

CRISANVER HOUSE

Set 2,000 feet above sea level in Vermont's Green Mountains, amid 120 acres of hiking trails, meadows, forests, ponds, and gardens, Crisanver House offers lots of options for exploring the natural beauty of the area. Opportunities abound year-round for lovers of outdoor activities, including hiking, golfing, snowshoeing, skiing, tennis, bocce ball, shuffleboard, and swimming on or near the premises.

1434 Crown Point Road
Shrewsbury, VT 05738
802-492-3589
www.crisanver.com

Cranberry-Orange Bread

This bread is great when spread with a little maple butter
and enjoyed with a cup of coffee.

Dutch Pancakes

When the batter for these pancakes hits the very hot pan,
it crawls up the sides of the pan, forming an edible bowl.

*At Crisanver House, breakfast is served in the conservatory with the Green Mountains as a
backdrop. This bed and breakfast prides itself on offering Vermont's natural bounty, using
locally sourced and organic food—some right from the inn's own garden—whenever possible.*

Cranberry-Orange Bread

Yields 1 loaf

2 cups all-purpose flour

2 teaspoons baking powder

½ teaspoon salt

½ teaspoon baking soda

¼ cup unsalted butter, at room
temperature

1 cup granulated sugar

1 large egg

1 tablespoon orange zest

½ cup chopped walnuts

½ cup orange juice

1½ cups fresh cranberries,
chopped coarse

1. Preheat the oven to 350°F. Grease and lightly flour a
9 x 5 x 3-inch loaf pan.

2. Sift the flour, baking powder, and salt together in
a bowl.

3. In another bowl, mix the baking soda and butter
together, then gradually blend in the sugar.

4. Beat in the egg, then stir in the orange zest and walnuts.

5. Add the flour mixture in thirds, alternating with the
orange juice.

6. Add the cranberries and blend them into the dough.

7. Pour the dough into the prepared loaf pan and bake for
1 hour and 20 minutes, or until a pick inserted in the
center comes out clean.

Dutch Pancakes

Yields 2 servings

4 large eggs

1 cup whole milk

½ teaspoon almond extract

1 cup all-purpose flour

Pinch of salt

4 tablespoons unsalted butter, melted

Confectioners' sugar and mint sprigs, for garnish

Warm maple syrup, for serving

Fresh fruit, for topping (optional)

1. Preheat the oven to 425°F. Put two 7-inch cast-iron pans in the oven to preheat.

2. With a mixer, beat the eggs, then add the milk and almond extract.

3. Add the flour and salt to the mixing bowl and beat until completely incorporated and smooth.

4. Mix in the melted butter.

5. Remove the pans from the oven and add a little butter to grease the bottom of each pan.

6. Quickly add half the batter to each pan and return to the oven. The batter will climb the sides of the pan, forming a cup. Cook until the pancakes are a golden color, about 7 to 10 minutes.

7. Remove the pancakes from the pans and put them on individual plates. Dust with confectioners' sugar, garnish with mint sprigs, and serve with warm maple syrup or top with fresh fruit, if desired.

Sweet Additions

Although Dutch Pancakes are delicious served just with warm maple syrup, you can dress them up a bit by topping them with fresh berries, melon, or other fruits and even a dollop of whipped cream.

THE INN AT ORMSBY HILL

This romantic inn, with such modern luxurious amenities as whirlpool tubs for two and fireplaces, also has a rich and colorful history. The oldest part of the Inn at Ormsby Hill dates back to 1764 and now contains the formal living room, gathering room, and former library, which is now a guest room. In the late 1800s, the home was owned by Edward Isham, a prominent Chicago attorney, whose friends in high places included his law partner, Robert Todd Lincoln, and President William Howard Taft. Isham, a great student of the Revolutionary War and the Green Mountain Boys, named the house Ormbsy Hill after Gideon Ormbsy, a Revolutionary War hero from Manchester.

1842 Main Street
Manchester Center, VT 05255
802-362-1163
www.ormsbyhill.com

House Specialties

Apple-Cheddar Quiche

This dish is a delicious combination of savory
and sweet and is perfect to serve in the fall.

Cinnamon-Maple Butter

With its quintessential Vermont flavor, this spread is great
on just about any bread or toast.

Raspberry-Goat Cheese Bread Pudding

All the work for this pudding is done the night before. In the morning,
just pop it in the oven and take time to enjoy your guests.

*The Inn at Ormsby Hill serves breakfast in the conservatory, which features a stunning
fireplace with an ornately carved European mantel and two walls of windows that afford
beautiful views of the grounds. Guests start the morning meal with steaming mugs of coffee
and fragrant mini loaves of Japanese bread baked fresh every morning.*

Apple-Cheddar Quiche

Yields 6 servings

1 10-inch pie crust

3 apples (any variety), peeled, cored, and diced

1½ tablespoons unsalted butter

1 cup grated sharp cheddar cheese (innkeeper's preference: Cabot)

3 large eggs plus 2 egg yolks

½ cup cottage cheese

1½ cups half-and-half

⅛ cup cinnamon sugar, or more to taste

Pinch of salt

1. Preheat the oven to 400°F. Partially bake the pie crust until the bottom begins to get golden, about 20 minutes. Set aside to cool and turn down the oven to 375°F, placing an oven rack in the lowest position.

2. In a large skillet, sauté the apples in the butter until slightly softened, 5 to 8 minutes.

3. Place the cooled pie crust on a cookie sheet. Place the apples in the bottom of the pie crust and top with the cheddar cheese.

4. In a large bowl, beat together the eggs, egg yolks, cottage cheese, and half-and-half. Pour this mixture over the apples and cheese in the pie crust.

5. Sprinkle with cinnamon sugar and salt.

6. Bake the quiche on the cookie sheet until the center is firm, about 40 to 55 minutes.

Cinnamon-Maple Butter

Yields 8 servings

½ cup (1 stick) unsalted butter, very soft

2 teaspoons cinnamon

2 tablespoons Vermont maple syrup

1. Using a wooden spoon, vigorously mix all the ingredients until well combined.

2. Fill butter molds, if desired, or simply roll the butter into a log, cover tightly with waxed paper, and freeze until ready to use, at least 2 hours.

3. Thaw for 30 minutes before using.

Raspberry-Goat Cheese Bread Pudding

Yields 8 servings

Note advance prep time.

Bread pudding:

1 medium loaf challah or other firm bread, cut into 1-inch cubes

5 large eggs, divided

2 cups whole milk

1 cup heavy cream

4 tablespoons granulated sugar, divided

2 teaspoons vanilla extract

½ teaspoon freshly grated nutmeg

½ teaspoon kosher salt

8 ounces goat cheese, softened

8 ounces mascarpone cheese

1½ jars (about 14 ounces) organic, seedless red raspberry fruit spread (innkeeper's preference: Santa Cruz brand)

Raspberry sauce:

1 pint fresh raspberries

Zest and juice from 1 lemon

1 cup granulated sugar

Garnish:

Fresh fruit (optional)

1. Grease a 13 x 9-inch baking dish and spread the bread cubes evenly over the bottom.

2. In a blender, combine 4 of the eggs with the milk, cream, 2 tablespoons of sugar, vanilla, nutmeg, and salt until smooth.

3. Pour the egg mixture evenly over the bread cubes, pushing down with a spatula for several minutes to help the bread absorb the liquid and make a firm base for the toppings.

4. Place the goat cheese, mascarpone, the remaining egg, and remaining 2 tablespoons of sugar in a medium bowl and beat with a hand mixer until the cheese is the consistency of cake frosting.

5. Spread the cheese mixture, like frosting, evenly over the bread. Spread the fruit spread in an even layer over the cheese.

6. Cover with plastic wrap, using toothpicks to keep the plastic from clinging to the fruit spread. Refrigerate overnight.

7. To make the raspberry sauce, combine the raspberries, lemon zest and juice, and sugar in a saucepan over low heat until the raspberries are broken down, about 6 to 7 minutes. Cool slightly.

8. Pour into a blender and purée until the sauce has thickened. Pour through a fine sieve to remove all the seeds.

9. Refrigerate the sauce until ready to use. (This sauce may be frozen for several months.)

10. In the morning, take the bread pudding out of the refrigerator and preheat the oven to 325°F.

11. Remove the plastic wrap and bake for 50 minutes, or until the cheese is lightly browned around the edges. Let sit for at least 10 minutes before cutting into squares.

12. Drizzle each serving with raspberry sauce and garnish with fresh fruit, if desired.

THE INN AT ROUND BARN FARM

The Inn at Round Barn Farm offers a mix of antique furnishings and unique architectural features, with the ultimate emphasis being on comfort and relaxation. On warm afternoons, tea is served on the terrace. The Mad River Valley, where the inn is located, offers four-season attractions for the sports enthusiast, arts lover, and shopper.

1661 East Warren Road
Waitsfield, VT 05673
802-496-2276
www.theroundbarn.com

House Specialties

Pumpkin Soufflé Pancakes

When misty summer mornings give way to mornings
with a nip in the air, these perfect fall pancakes make their way onto
the Round Barn griddle and usher in the new season.

Hot Apple Compote

This apple compote is a great topping for French toast and pancakes of all types
as well as an excellent filling for apple strudel. You can also add ½ cup of dried
cranberries for a beautiful color contrast and extra flavor kick.

Tomato Jam

Tomato jam is a truly useful condiment to have around the house.
At the inn, it's served at breakfast with cheddar scones and on Vermont cheese
boards (it lends itself especially to creamy, brie-like cheeses). Adding some chili
powder and a hint of clove makes this little jam stand up to flavorful meats,
and adding Dijon mustard will make it even heartier. Experiment
with the recipe to find your own favorite blend.

Maple Sausage and Apple Torta

Making your own sausage is not difficult, and the flavor payoff
is well worth it. You can use this mixture as bulk sausage for the torta
or shape it into patties and fry.

Pumpkin Soufflé Pancakes

Yields 12 4-inch pancakes

1 cup whole milk

⅔ cup pumpkin purée

2 large eggs

⅓ cup vegetable oil

½ teaspoon vanilla extract

1 cup all-purpose flour

2 teaspoons baking powder

½ teaspoon cinnamon

½ teaspoon allspice

½ teaspoon nutmeg

Hot Apple Compote (below),
  for serving

1. Combine the milk, pumpkin, eggs, oil, and vanilla in a large bowl.

2. Combine the flour, baking powder, cinnamon, allspice, and nutmeg in a smaller bowl.

3. Slowly stir the flour mixture into the pumpkin mixture until well blended.

4. Spoon ⅓ cup of batter for each pancake onto a medium-hot greased griddle or skillet.

5. Cook for 3 to 4 minutes per side. Do not flip the pancakes until the edges are firm or they will fall apart.

6. Serve with the compote.

Hot Apple Compote

Yields 5 cups

¼ cup (½ stick) salted butter

6 tart apples, peeled, cored,
  and sliced ½ inch thick

¼ cup apple cider, apple juice,
  or water

¼ cup granulated sugar

Zest of 1 lemon

1 teaspoon grated ginger
  (optional)

1. Melt the butter in a sauté pan over medium heat. Add the apples, apple cider, sugar, lemon zest, and ginger, if using.

2. Cook, covered, for 15 minutes, or until the apples are soft but still firm.

Tomato Jam

Yields about 4 cups

6 cups tomatoes, peeled,
    seeded, diced, and drained of
    excess liquid

3½ cups granulated sugar

Zest and juice of 1 lemon

1 cinnamon stick

1. Combine all the ingredients in a nonreactive (stainless-steel or glass) pot over medium to low heat, stirring frequently to prevent scorching. Cook for 1 hour, or until the mixture thickens.

2. Transfer to sterile Mason jars and process in boiling water for 10 minutes (be careful to follow proper canning technique and procedures). Alternatively, allow to cool and store in a tightly closed container in the refrigerator for up to 2 weeks.

Things to Do

Take a Signature Vermont Foodie Tour

In close proximity to the Inn at Round Barn Farm are several renowned culinary hot spots. Plan to visit the New England Culinary Institute, Ben & Jerry's ice cream factory, the Cabot Cheese factory, and Cold Hollow Cider Mill to see where some of Vermont's favorite foods are made.

Maple Sausage and Apple Torta

Yields 8 to 10 servings

Sausage:

1 pound ground pork

3 tablespoons Vermont maple syrup

1 teaspoon salt

½ teaspoon sage

½ teaspoon cardamom

¼ teaspoon black pepper

¼ teaspoon ground ginger

⅛ teaspoon dill weed

⅛ teaspoon mace

Torta:

1 tablespoon salted butter

1½ cups apples, peeled and chopped

2¼ cups whole milk

6 large eggs

⅓ cup Vermont maple syrup

1 teaspoon nutmeg

16 to 20 ½-inch-thick slices French bread

1. Preheat the oven to 350°F.

2. Combine all the sausage ingredients in a bowl and mix until thoroughly blended.

3. Brown ¾ pound of the sausage in a medium skillet over medium-high heat, stirring until crumbly. Drain and set aside. (Reserve the rest of the sausage for another use.)

4. To make the torta, melt the butter in a large skillet and sauté the apples until tender. Remove from the heat and stir in the cooked sausage.

5. Combine the milk, eggs, maple syrup, and nutmeg in a bowl, mixing well.

6. Grease a 9-inch springform pan and cover the outside bottom of the pan with foil to prevent leaking.

7. Dip 8 to 10 slices of bread in the egg mixture and arrange them on the bottom of the prepared pan, overlapping the slices and leaving no spaces in between.

8. Spoon the sausage and apple mixture on top of the bread. Dip the remaining slices of bread in the egg mixture and layer them over the sausage mixture.

9. Pour any remaining egg mixture over the top and press down slightly with a spatula. (The torta can be prepared in advance up to this point. Refrigerate, covered, overnight).

10. Bake uncovered for 1 hour, or until a knife inserted in the center comes out clean and the top is golden brown. Cut into pie-shaped wedges to serve.

Sweet Additions

Although delicious by itself, the Maple Sausage and
Apple Torta is even better when served with this concoction
of maple syrup and apples. Combine 1 cup of maple syrup,
1 cup of diced apples, and a cinnamon stick. Simmer for
20 minutes and spoon over the warm torta.

THE INN AT WESTON

The emphasis at the Inn at Weston is on relaxation. Several garden areas, a deck, and a gazebo provide guests with appealing spots to curl up with a good book or sip a glass of wine and enjoy the pastoral scenery. The inn also offers its guests pet-friendly lodging. Lexi, the resident golden retriever, loves to make new canine friends. There are numerous activities nearby that are dog-friendly, and the innkeepers will gladly point you in the right direction.

630 Main Street, Route 100
Weston, VT 05161
802-824-6789
www.innweston.com

House Specialties

Potato, Leek, and Taylor Farm Gouda Frittata

The innkeepers like to use local ingredients whenever possible.
This frittata is made with cheese from nearby Taylor Farm,
but if you can't get that, just use your favorite Gouda.

Inn at Weston Granola

This is the inn's most requested recipe. You can experiment with the taste by
adding any dried fruits in whatever combination you like.

*In the morning, guests at the Inn at Weston are greeted by a bountiful sideboard
laden with fresh fruit, homemade muffins, coffee cake, granola, and more.*

Potato, Leek, and Taylor Farm Gouda Frittata

Yields 4 servings

4 tablespoons extra-virgin olive oil, divided

¼ cup (½ stick) unsalted butter, divided

3 medium leeks, sliced, soaked in cold water to remove any dirt, and dried on paper towels

Salt and pepper

3 medium Yukon gold potatoes, cut in half, boiled until soft, and drained

8 medium eggs, whisked with 2 tablespoons half-and-half

1 cup grated Taylor Farm Gouda cheese (or other Gouda of your choice)

Parsley, for garnish

1. Preheat the broiler.

2. Heat 2 tablespoons of olive oil and 2 tablespoons of the butter in a large skillet and sauté the leeks until golden, about 5 minutes. Season with salt and pepper and set aside.

3. Divide the remaining olive oil and butter between 4 6-inch ovenproof omelet pans over medium heat. Add the potatoes and sauté for about 3 minutes, or until warm.

4. Divide and add the leeks to the pans and continue cooking for another 2 minutes.

5. Add the egg mixture and more salt and pepper, if desired.

6. Lift the corners of the eggs as they set and let any uncooked egg run under until the top is not runny and the bottom is thoroughly cooked.

7. Sprinkle Gouda over the top of the eggs and place the pans under the broiler for 30 seconds, or until the cheese is melted.

8. Garnish with parsley and serve.

■ ■ ■ ■ ■ ■ ■ ■ ■ ■ ■

Tasty Tidbit

Taylor Farm, the source of the cheese for the frittata, is Vermont's only Gouda producer. This 180-year-old dairy farm specializes in handcrafted raw-milk farmstead cheeses. Among their signature cheeses are Vermont Farmstead Gouda, Maple Smoked Farmstead Gouda, and several flavored Goudas. Visit their website (www.taylorfarmvermont.com) for more information.

■ ■ ■ ■ ■ ■ ■ ■ ■ ■ ■

Inn at Weston Granola

Yields about 10 cups

3 cups old-fashioned oats (innkeeper's preference: Quaker)

1 cup sweetened flaked coconut

1 cup sliced almonds

5 tablespoons honey (local, if available), or more to taste

¾ cup canola oil

½ cup dried cranberries

½ cup dried cherries

½ cup dried apricots

½ cup raisins

½ cup whole roasted cashews (unsalted)

1. Preheat the oven to 350°F.

2. In a large bowl, mix the oats, coconut, and almonds.

3. Whisk the honey into the canola oil and pour over the oat mixture. Mix well.

4. Spread on a baking sheet and bake, stirring occasionally, for 20 to 30 minutes, or until golden brown and dry.

5. Stir the mixture while it is hot out of the oven so it doesn't stick together. Allow to cool.

6. Add the dried fruits and nuts.

Things to Do

Learn About Orchids

A unique feature of the Inn at Weston is a state-of-the-art greenhouse that contains a large collection of orchids. One of the innkeepers has been collecting the plants for over twenty years and has lectured widely in New England about the evolution and biology of these beautiful flowers, as well as how to grow them in a home environment. Guests are encouraged to bring orchids that need repotting—or even "sick" orchids—to the inn for help.

RABBIT HILL INN

Back in the late 1700s, Lower Waterford was the halfway point on the trade route between Montreal, Canada, and the busy American harbors of Portland, Maine, and Boston, Massachusetts. An enterprising man, Samuel Hodby founded a tavern where weary travelers and loggers working on the nearby Connecticut River could stop off and enjoy a meal, pick up provisions, and stay over to rest. Today, the tradition of hospitality continues, and guests enjoy canopy beds, fireplaces, whirlpool tubs, and lots of little extras that create the perfect romantic getaway.

48 Lower Waterford Road
Lower Waterford, VT 05848
802-748-5168
www.rabbithillinn.com

House Specialties

Vermont Cheddar Egg Strudel with Spinach Cream

Vermont's Cabot cheese is well known and widely available, but if you can't find it, use a good sharp cheddar for this recipe.

Bacon Jam

This bacon jam recipe will become one of your favorites. Try this delicious, savory (and somewhat addictive) jam with breakfasts, entrées, cheese and crackers, and appetizers. Once you start experimenting with it, you'll always want to have a jar on hand.

Maple-Caramel-Pumpkin Upside-Down Cakes

You can bake this dish in ramekins to be served individually or in a large cake pan to be cut and shared.

Breakfast Corn Chowder with Poached Eggs

On the way to work one very cold morning, the inn's pastry chef came up with the concept for this hearty, delicious winter dish. An instant hit, it soon became one of the inn's signature dishes. If you eliminate the bacon, it makes a great vegetarian breakfast dish, too.

Vermont Cheddar Egg Strudel with Spinach Cream

Yields 4 to 6 servings

¼ cup canola oil

12 large eggs, beaten with ½ cup heavy cream

1 sheet puff pastry, at room temperature

½ cup shredded Vermont sharp cheddar cheese (innkeeper's preference: Cabot)

2 tablespoons unsalted butter, melted

1 cup fresh spinach, blanched

1 cup heavy cream

Salt and pepper

1. Preheat a convection oven to 350°F (400°F for a conventional oven).

2. Heat the oil in a large nonstick sauté pan over medium heat.

3. Cook the egg mixture over medium-high heat, scrambling until barely set.

4. On a small baking sheet, lay out the puff pastry.

5. Place the eggs in a line straight along the center of the pastry.

6. Top with the cheese and roll the pastry into a cylinder.

7. Brush with butter and bake until golden brown, about 20 to 25 minutes.

8. While the strudel is baking, purée the spinach with heavy cream in a blender or food processor.

9. Pour the spinach-cream mixture into a medium saucepan and simmer over low heat until reduced by one-third in volume, about 5 minutes.

10. Season with salt and pepper.

11. Spoon the hot spinach-cream sauce over the freshly baked strudel and serve immediately.

Bacon Jam

Yields 3 cups

½ pound bacon, diced

2 onions, diced

4 garlic cloves, minced

2 apples, peeled and diced

½ cup apple cider vinegar

½ cup dark brown sugar, packed

¼ cup maple syrup

¾ cup strong brewed coffee

1 teaspoon black pepper, or more to taste

1. Cook the bacon in a medium skillet until crispy. Drain the fat, reserving 2 tablespoons.

2. Add the onion, garlic, and apples to the pan with the bacon and the reserved bacon fat. Cook until everything is tender, about 5 to 10 minutes.

3. Add the vinegar, brown sugar, maple syrup, coffee, and pepper and cook until thick and syrupy, about 5 minutes. Cool slightly at room temperature.

4. Place the cooled mixture in a food processor and process until the jam reaches a spreadable consistency.

5. Store in an airtight container in the refrigerator for up to 2 weeks.

Maple-Caramel-Pumpkin Upside-Down Cakes

Yields 8 individual servings or 1 9-inch round cake

1 cup maple syrup

8 tablespoons unsalted butter, divided

¼ cup heavy cream

⅓ cup granulated sugar

½ cup dark brown sugar, packed

½ cup pumpkin purée

1 large egg

½ teaspoon cinnamon

¼ teaspoon ground cloves

¼ teaspoon ginger

⅛ teaspoon salt

½ teaspoon baking powder

¼ teaspoon baking soda

1 cup all-purpose flour

⅓ cup buttermilk

Sweetened whipped cream, for serving

1. Preheat the oven to 325°F. Grease 8 ramekins or 1 9-inch round cake pan.

2. Boil the maple syrup until it reaches 240°F, or soft-ball stage on a candy thermometer.

3. Add 2 tablespoons of the butter and the heavy cream and cook for 3 minutes on medium heat to caramelize.

4. Pour the maple syrup mixture into the greased ramekins or cake pan.

5. Chill in the refrigerator while mixing the cake batter.

6. Cream the remaining butter and the sugars together until there are no lumps.

7. Add the pumpkin purée and egg and mix.

8. Add the cinnamon, cloves, ginger, salt, baking powder, baking soda, flour, and buttermilk and mix until well incorporated.

9. Spoon the batter into the ramekins or pour into the cake pan. Bake in the ramekins for 30 minutes, or in the cake pan for 45 to 50 minutes, or until the top of the cakes are firm to the touch.

10. Let sit for 3 to 5 minutes before turning out the cakes onto plates.

11. Serve warm with sweetened whipped cream.

Breakfast Corn Chowder with Poached Eggs

Yields 6 servings

1 tablespoon vegetable oil

¼ pound bacon, diced

4 cups vegetable stock

3 cups diced red potatoes

1 onion, diced

½ cup diced celery

1 cup diced fennel

1 cup cooked fresh or frozen corn

¼ cup diced red bell pepper

2 teaspoons minced fresh rosemary

1 tablespoon flour

2 cups half-and-half

Salt and pepper

6 slices toasted baguette

12 poached eggs

12 slices cooked bacon and 6 rosemary sprigs, for garnish

Rosemary oil, for drizzling

1. Put the oil and bacon in a soup pot over medium heat.

2. At the same time, put the stock and potatoes in a separate pot, bring to a simmer over low heat, and cook until the potatoes are just tender, about 10 minutes.

3. When the bacon is just crisp, add the onion, celery, and fennel to the soup pot. Cook until tender, about 10 minutes.

4. Add the corn, bell pepper, and rosemary. Stir and remove from the heat. Sprinkle flour over the vegetables and stir again.

5. At this point, add the potatoes and stock to the bacon and vegetable mixture. Return to the heat and slowly bring to a simmer while stirring.

6. Add the half-and-half and season with salt and pepper. Bring back to a simmer.

7. To serve, ladle the chowder into a warmed bowl. Place a toasted baguette slice on top of the chowder and gently place two poached eggs on top of the toast. Garnish with two slices of warm bacon and place a sprig of fresh rosemary between the eggs. For extra flavor, drizzle the top of the eggs with rosemary oil (olive oil infused with rosemary).

WEST MOUNTAIN INN

The century-old West Mountain Inn is set on 150 acres on a mountainside overlooking the Battenkill Valley. The rooms feature antique furnishings, where guests can relax after a day of skiing or outlet shopping and enjoy the spectacular mountain views. When it comes to dining, the emphasis is on seasonal recipes prepared with farm-fresh local ingredients.

144 West Mountain Inn Road
Arlington, VT 05250
802-375-6516
www.westmountaininn.com

House Specialties

Ooey Gooey

This guest favorite, made with eggs from a local farm,
Vermont cheddar cheese, and Aunt Min's homemade
Swedish rye bread, is super simple and oh, so satisfying.

Aunt Min's Rye Bread

Passed down from the original innkeeper's aunt, this recipe
has been a standard at the inn for many years.

Sticky Buns

This recipe requires a bit of time for prepping and rising but the delicious end
result is well worth the effort.

Tasty Tidbit

West Mountain Inn is a part of Vermont Fresh Network (www.vermontfresh.
net), a group dedicated to bringing fresh, flavorful, high-quality food to all
Vermonters and visitors by offering programs and information to connect
farmers, food producers, and chefs who support Vermont agriculture.

Ooey Gooey

Yields 2 servings

2 slices Aunt Min's Rye
   Bread (below)

4 large eggs

2 tablespoons mayonnaise

Dash of paprika

1 ounce sharp cheddar
   cheese, shredded

1. Preheat the broiler.
2. Toast the bread.
3. Fry the eggs sunny-side up.
4. Spread the mayonnaise on the toast.
5. Place the eggs on top and sprinkle with paprika and cheese.
6. Broil a minute or so until the cheese is melted.

Aunt Min's Rye Bread

Yields 3 loaves

4 tablespoons active dry yeast

2 cups warm water (110°F.)

1 cup salted butter, melted

½ cup dark brown sugar,
   packed

¼ teaspoon salt

½ cup fennel seeds

½ cup molasses

2 cups rye flour

8 cups bread flour
   (all-purpose flour
   works, too)

1. Combine the yeast and warm water in the bowl of an electric mixer and let stand for 5 minutes.
2. Add the butter, brown sugar, salt, fennel seeds, molasses, and rye flour. Begin mixing with the dough hook and add the bread flour 2 cups at a time, until a soft dough forms. Continue mixing with the dough hook, adding flour as needed, until the dough forms a ball around the dough hook and is not sticking to the bowl, about 8 to 10 minutes.
3. Butter the inside of a large bowl, put in the dough, and let rise until doubled, about 1 hour.
4. Preheat the oven to 350°F.
5. Shape the dough into 3 oval loaves and let rise again until doubled in size, about 30 minutes.
6. Place the loaves on a greased baking sheet or in greased loaf pans and bake for 35 minutes, or until the bread is golden brown and sounds hollow when tapped.

Sticky Buns

Yields 12 sticky buns

Note advance prep time.

2 tablespoons active dry yeast

½ cup warm water (110°F.)

¼ cup granulated sugar

1¼ cups buttermilk

2 large eggs

¾ cup (1½ sticks) unsalted butter, softened, divided

4 cups all-purpose flour, plus up to 1 additional cup if needed to get the right dough consistency

1 teaspoon baking powder

1 teaspoon salt

¼ cup cinnamon sugar

½ cup light brown sugar, packed

1 cup pecans, coarsely chopped

½ cup maple syrup

1. In the bowl of an electric mixer, combine the yeast, warm water, and sugar and let sit for 10 minutes.

2. Add the buttermilk and eggs and mix well with the dough hook attachment.

3. Add ¼ cup of the butter and continue mixing.

4. In a separate bowl, combine the flour, baking powder, and salt.

5. Add the flour mixture to the yeast mixture, 2 cups at a time, with the mixer set at medium speed. The dough should be fairly soft, but smooth. If the dough is too loose, add more flour.

6. Knead the dough with a dough hook for 10 minutes until the dough is not sticky and forms a ball around the dough hook. Put it in a greased bowl and let rise until doubled, about 1 hour.

7. Punch the dough down and roll it out to a rectangle about ¼ inch thick. Spread with ¼ cup of butter and sprinkle with cinnamon sugar. Roll up lengthwise, like a jellyroll. Be sure to squeeze the dough together firmly.

8. Spread the brown sugar, pecans, ¼ cup of butter, and maple syrup in the bottom of a 13 x 9-inch baking pan.

9. Cut the rolled dough into ¾-inch slices and place in the pan cut-sides up. Cover with plastic wrap and let rise until doubled, about 45 minutes.

10. Preheat the oven to 350°F.

11. Bake 15 to 20 minutes, until lightly brown. Let cool slightly, then remove one cinnamon roll at a time and turn over onto a plate so the caramel sauce is on top. Spoon any sauce left in the bottom of the pan over the rolls and serve.

THE WILDFLOWER INN

All the homey hospitality of a bed and breakfast with the amenities of a resort—that's what's offered at the Wildflower Inn. Set on 300 acres in Vermont's Northeast Kingdom, the inn offers onsite four-season attractions for everyone, including swimming, ice-skating, hiking, mountain biking, sledding, and more. The guest rooms are lodged in a variety of separate buildings, making the inn ideal for both family vacations and romantic getaways. Canine guests are welcome as well.

The Wildflower Inn
New England's Country Resort

2059 Darling Hill Road
Lyndonville, VT 05851
802-626-8310
www.wildflowerinn.com

Maple Granola

This granola is sweetened with a signature Vermont food product: maple syrup.

Tasty Tidbit

Legend has it that, after returning from a hunting trip, a Native American chief threw his tomahawk into a sugar maple. Sap from the tree ran down the trunk and into a birch-bark container that had been left there. The chief's wife, thinking the sap was water, poured it into a pot with some meat she was cooking. As the "water" boiled away, a sweet glaze with a delicious flavor was left on the meat. The rest, as they say, is history.

Maple Granola

Yields about 25 cups

20 cups old-fashioned oats

2 cups shredded unsweetened coconut

1 pound pecans, chopped coarse

1½ cups pure Vermont maple syrup

3 cups molasses

Raisins, to taste (optional)

1. Preheat the oven to 300°F.

2. Mix the oats, coconut, and pecans together in a large bowl.

3. Add the maple syrup and molasses and toss well to evenly coat the mixture.

4. Spread the mixture evenly onto 2 sheet pans. Bake for approximately 1 hour, stirring every 15 minutes, until golden brown.

5. Add the raisins, if using, after the granola has cooled. Store in an airtight container in a cool, dry place for 2 to 4 weeks.

Tasty Tidbit

Vermonters celebrate the maple-sugaring season in a unique way: by eating a combination of maple syrup, plain raised donuts, and dill pickles! After every two or three bites of donut dipped in maple syrup, they take a bite of dill pickle. The reasoning behind this unusual tradition? Those who partake in it say that the sweet and sour tastes bring out the best in each other.

Discover the Maple Sugaring Process

It takes forty gallons of sap to make a single gallon of maple syrup. According the United States Department of Agriculture, Vermont is by far the largest producer of maple syrup in the country, with 42 percent of total production—or 1,320,000 gallons—at last count.

Conditions have to be just right for the maple sap to flow: warm, sunny days with temperatures rising above 40°F and freezing temperatures at night. The maple-sugaring season in Vermont's Northeast Kingdom usually runs from sometime in late February until early April, for a total of four to six weeks, depending on the weather and temperature conditions.

During the sugaring season, many sugarhouses offer tours and programs. In late March, the state of Vermont hosts the Maple Open House Weekend, with sugarhouses and restaurants offering a variety of educational and tasting activities related to maple syrup. Many sugarhouses are open year-round. Visit www.vermontmaple.org for a current listing of related events.

Sap is collected from the maple trees and boiled down to make maple syrup.

WOODSTOCK INN AND RESORT

Set in a quintessential New England town, the Woodstock Inn and Resort offers rustic country décor with modern comfort and amenities. Guests can enjoy browsing the shops on the quaint main street or more active pursuits like skiing, biking, and golf. An onsite spa offers a plethora of relaxing treatments and services.

14 The Green
Woodstock, VT 05091
802-457-1100
www.woodstockinn.com

Baked Cinnamon-Apple French Toast

This dish is delicious any time of the year, but it's particularly enjoyable on cool fall mornings when apples are at their peak and the first hint of cold is in the air.

Chocolate Waffles

Chocolate waffles are great for breakfast or dessert.
You can top them with fresh fruit, maple syrup, your favorite ice cream,
or, for a really decadent finish, drizzle them with chocolate sauce.

Local Color

With "leaf-peeping" being one of Vermont's greatest fall
attractions, a helpful resource is the Vermont Foliage Guide
(www.virtualvermonter.com/foliage.htm). This handy website offers
biweekly foliage reports and peak time predictors, suggested scenic
foliage drives, and even foliage webcams so you can check on the
color yourself and plan your visit accordingly.

Baked Cinnamon-Apple French Toast

Yields 8 to 12 servings

Note advance prep time.

7 slices Texas toast, cut into large cubes

⅓ cup light brown sugar, packed

1 teaspoon cinnamon

½ teaspoon nutmeg

2 tablespoons salted butter

2 small McIntosh apples, peeled and diced into 1-inch pieces

2 small Granny Smith apples, peeled and diced into 1-inch pieces

6 large eggs

⅓ cup granulated sugar

2 cups whole milk

2 teaspoons vanilla extract

1. Preheat the oven to 200°F.

2. Place the cubes of Texas toast onto baking sheets and place in the oven, stirring occasionally until dry but not browned, about 5 minutes

3. In a bowl, combine the brown sugar, cinnamon, and nutmeg and set aside.

4. Heat a deep skillet. Once hot, add the butter and brown.

5. Add the apples to the browned butter and cook until the apples just begin to turn soft, about 5 minutes. Add the brown sugar and spice mixture and cook for 1 minute more.

6. Remove from the heat and allow to cool.

7. Meanwhile, combine the eggs, sugar, milk, and vanilla and purée with a blender stick or whisk until very smooth.

8. Coat a 13 x 9-inch baking dish with vegetable cooking spray and spread the Texas toast cubes to cover the bottom of the dish.

9. Pour the egg mixture over the bread cubes and let them soak up the liquid. Mix the bread around once and press down into the liquid with a spatula to help absorb.

10. Spoon the cooled apple mixture over the top of the bread in the baking dish, cover, and refrigerate overnight.

11. In the morning, preheat the oven to 300°F.

12. Uncover and bake the French toast for 1½ hours, or until puffed and golden. After the first half-hour, rotate the pan. After the second half-hour, cover with a piece of foil that has been coated with vegetable cooking spray on the food contact side.

13. Allow to sit for 10 minutes, then slice into squares and serve.

Chocolate Waffles

Yields about 16 waffles

3 cups all-purpose flour

6 tablespoons granulated sugar

1 cup cocoa powder

2 teaspoons baking powder

2 teaspoons salt

1 teaspoon baking soda

6 large eggs, beaten

2 teaspoons vanilla extract

2 cups buttermilk, plus more
   if needed to thin batter

½ cup (1 stick) salted
   butter, melted

Chocolate sauce, for
   garnish (optional)

1. Combine the flour, sugar, cocoa powder, baking powder, salt, and baking soda in a large bowl.

2. Whisk the eggs, vanilla, and buttermilk in a separate bowl.

3. Add the egg mixture to the flour mixture and mix until all the wet ingredients are incorporated into the dry.

4. Mix in the melted butter.

5. If the batter is too thick to ladle, thin it with some extra buttermilk.

6. Bake in a Belgian waffle iron, according to manufacturer's directions. Garnish with chocolate sauce, if desired.

Blair Hill Inn

Noble
House
Inn

The Kingsleigh Inn

Brewster
House

The
Oxford
House
Inn

Five Gables Inn

The Captain Lord Mansion

Maine

Maine is a joy in the summer.
But the soul of Maine is more
apparent in the winter.

—Paul Theroux

BLAIR HILL INN

Set high atop a hill on a fifteen-acre estate, this circa 1891 inn has impressive views of Moosehead Lake and the surrounding mountains. Blair Hill Inn has its own greenhouse, catch-and-release trout pond and onsite fly-fishing instruction, and beautifully landscaped grounds and gardens. A variety of outdoor excursions, including seaplane rides, hiking, and kayaking, are all available nearby.

351 Lily Bay Road
Greenville, ME 04441
207-695-0224
www.blairhill.com

House Specialties

Bubbling Grapefruit with Warm Maine Blueberries

This simple dish comes as a delightful surprise when served
as a breakfast starter course on cool Maine mornings.

Crispy Maine Potato Stack

The outside of the potato stack is crispy, and the inside
is tender and scrumptious with herbs and melted cheese.

Spicy Maine Crab Cakes "Eggs Benedict" with Lemon Aioli

Enjoy this Down-East version of a breakfast classic.

Bubbling Grapefruit with Warm Maine Blueberries

Yields 8 servings

4 grapefruit, cut in half and sectioned

8 teaspoons light brown sugar

1 cup frozen wild Maine blueberries

8 fresh mint leaves, for garnish (optional)

1. Preheat the broiler.

2. Place the grapefruit halves faceup on a broiler pan. Spread about 1 teaspoon of brown sugar on top of each half.

3. Place the grapefruit halves into the oven and broil until the edges of the grapefruit begin to brown and the sugar is bubbling, about 3 to 4 minutes.

4. While the grapefruit halves are cooking, warm the blueberries in a small saucepan over medium-low heat for about 5 minutes.

5. Remove the grapefruit from the oven and place each half in a small bowl or on a plate. Spoon a teaspoonful of the hot blueberries and their juice on top. Garnish each half with a mint leaf, if desired, and serve piping hot.

Tasty Tidbit

What makes wild Maine blueberries different from other blueberries? Wild blueberries are much smaller than their cultivated cousins. Don't be fooled by the small size, however. Wild blueberries have a more intense flavor and, because most of the nutrients are in the skins, wild blueberries have twice as many antioxidants per serving as cultivated blueberries.

Crispy Maine Potato Stack

Yields 8 servings

4 medium Maine russet potatoes, peeled

3 tablespoons duck fat (clarified butter can be used as a substitute), divided

Salt and pepper

⅛ teaspoon herbes de Provence

3 tablespoons blue cheese

1. Use a mandolin to thinly slice each potato.

2. Melt 2 tablespoons of duck fat in a medium skillet over medium heat.

3. Place 2 layers of potatoes in concentric circles in the bottom of the skillet. Turn the heat down to low.

4. Season with salt and pepper. Dust with herbes de Provence and sprinkle with half the blue cheese. Add another layer of potatoes, then more herbs and cheese. End with a layer of potatoes.

5. Melt the remaining duck fat in a microwave and drizzle over the top of the potatoes.

6. Cook for about 20 minutes. Loosen the potato stack, flip, and cook on the other side for about 20 minutes, or until each side is very brown and crispy. (For an easy way to flip the potato stack, slide it onto a plate, then turn it over and slide it back into the pan.)

7. Remove to a cutting board and slice into 8 wedges.

■ ■ ■ ■ ■ ■ ■ ■ ■ ■ ■ ■ ■ ■

Tasty Tidbit

Back in the 1940s, Maine was the top grower of potatoes in the entire country. Today, the state ranks around tenth. However, potato demand is still going strong: The average person consumes 117 pounds of potatoes per year—17 of them in the form of potato chips.

■ ■ ■ ■ ■ ■ ■ ■ ■ ■ ■ ■ ■ ■

Spicy Maine Crab Cakes "Eggs Benedict" with Lemon Aioli

Yields 10 crab cakes (5 servings)

2 tablespoons olive oil

1 cup minced Vidalia onion

½ cup minced celery

½ cup minced red pepper

½ cup minced green pepper

¼ cup minced jalapeño pepper

1½ teaspoons Old Bay seasoning

1 tablespoon minced garlic

1 pound fresh Maine crabmeat, squeezed
  dry and slightly shredded

¼ cup sliced scallions

¼ cup grated Parmesan cheese

3 tablespoons spicy whole-grain mustard

3 tablespoons freshly squeezed lemon juice

½ cup mayonnaise

1 teaspoon Worcestershire sauce

½ teaspoon Tabasco sauce

3 egg yolks

1 cup breadcrumbs

10 tomato slices and 1 recipe
  Lemon Aioli (page 221), for serving

10 large eggs, poached or fried to
  desired doneness

1. Preheat the oven to 350°F.

2. Heat the olive oil in a large skillet over medium-high heat. Sauté the onion, celery, and red, green, and jalapeño peppers. Add the Old Bay seasoning and sauté until the vegetables are soft and slightly browned, about 5 minutes. Add the garlic and cook another 2 minutes. Let cool for 5 minutes.

3. In a large bowl, combine the crabmeat, scallions, cheese, mustard, and lemon juice.

4. In a separate bowl, mix the mayonnaise, Worcestershire, Tabasco, and egg yolks.

5. Combine the vegetable and crab mixtures.

6. Fold in the mayonnaise mixture and ¾ cup of breadcrumbs.

7. Divide into 10 equal patty-sized portions and pat with the remaining breadcrumbs.

8. Heat a grill pan, grease with olive oil, and add the crab cakes. Cook until golden brown on each side, about 3 minutes per side, then place in the oven for 5 minutes to finish cooking.

9. For each serving, place 2 crab cakes on tomato slices and top each one with a dollop of aioli and a poached or fried egg.

Lemon Aioli

½ cup mayonnaise

1 garlic clove, minced

1 tablespoon chopped chives

3 tablespoons freshly squeezed lemon juice

½ teaspoon lemon zest

Kosher salt and freshly ground pepper

1. Place the mayonnaise, garlic, chives, lemon juice, and lemon zest in a bowl, season with salt and pepper to taste, and whisk until smooth.

BREWSTER HOUSE

Close to L. L. Bean and Freeport outlet shopping as well as the Maine coast, this bed and breakfast is ideally situated for shopaholics and beachcombers alike. Built in the late nineteenth century, when Freeport was first becoming prosperous, the inn reflects the hallmarks of solid craftsmanship and elegant appointments. Period details include cypress floors, bay windows, a mahogany mantelpiece, and, of course, a porch to rock on as you sip iced tea and take in the beautifully landscaped yard.

180 Main Street
Freeport, ME 04032
207-865-4121
www.brewsterhouse.com

Lemon-Ricotta Stuffed French Toast with Wild Maine Blueberry Compote

The tang of lemon and the sweetness of blueberries are
a winning flavor combination in this French toast.

Orange-Pecan French Toast

This rich and decadent breakfast dish gets prepared the night before.
In the morning, no work for the host or hostess; simply bake and enjoy.

Tasty Tidbit

Over 90 percent of the wild blueberries harvested
in the United States come from Maine.

Lemon-Ricotta Stuffed French Toast with Wild Maine Blueberry Compote

Yields 6 servings

6 large croissants

4 ounces cream cheese

2 tablespoons granulated sugar

2 teaspoons freshly squeezed lemon juice

2 teaspoons grated lemon zest, plus more for garnish

⅛ teaspoon pure vanilla extract

¾ cup whole-milk ricotta cheese

4 large eggs

½ cup heavy cream

Confectioners' sugar, for garnish

Fresh blueberries and Wild Maine Blueberry Compote (page 225), for serving

1. Preheat the oven to 375°F. Cover a cookie sheet with parchment paper.

2. Slice the croissants in half lengthwise.

3. Mix together the cream cheese, sugar, lemon juice, lemon zest, and vanilla.

4. Stir the ricotta into the cream cheese mixture.

5. Spread 2 tablespoons of the cream cheese filling between the croissant halves to make a sandwich.

6. Whisk together the eggs and heavy cream.

7. Preheat the griddle and grease with butter.

8. Dip the croissant sandwiches in the egg mixture, allowing the excess to drip off before placing the croissants on the griddle. Brown the croissants, about 3 to 4 minutes per side.

9. Place the browned croissants on the parchment-lined cookie sheet and bake for 8 to 10 minutes, or until the cheese filling is heated through.

10. Sprinkle with confectioners' sugar and lemon zest.

11. Serve with fresh blueberries and warm blueberry compote.

Wild Maine Blueberry Compote

Yields 1½ cups (enough for 6 servings of French toast)

2 cups wild Maine
   blueberries, fresh
   or frozen

½ cup granulated sugar

2 teaspoons freshly
   squeezed lemon juice

1. Combine the blueberries and sugar in a saucepan over low heat and stir constantly until the sugar dissolves, about 2 to 3 minutes.

2. Add the lemon juice and bring to a boil. Lower the heat and simmer for another 2 minutes.

3. Serve warm. Compote can be stored, covered, in the refrigerator for up to 2 days.

Orange-Pecan French Toast

Yields 8 to 12 servings

Note advance prep time.

1¼ cups brown sugar, packed

½ cup (1 stick) salted butter

2 tablespoons light corn syrup

⅓ cup chopped pecans

1 teaspoon grated orange zest

1 cup orange juice

1 tablespoon Grand Marnier

½ cup whole milk

3 tablespoons granulated sugar

5 large eggs

1 teaspoon pure vanilla extract

1 teaspoon cinnamon

1 loaf (1 pound) French bread

Crème fraîche or whipped cream, confectioners' sugar, and raspberries, for garnish

1. Coat a 13 x 9-inch baking dish with vegetable cooking spray and set aside.

2. Combine the brown sugar, butter, and corn syrup in a saucepan over medium-low heat. Stir until the butter and sugar have melted together to form a caramel sauce, about 5 minutes.

3. Pour the caramel sauce into the prepared baking dish. Sprinkle the pecans over the caramel sauce.

4. Place the orange zest, orange juice, Grand Marnier, milk, sugar, eggs, vanilla, and cinnamon in a large mixing bowl and mix with an electric mixer until blended together.

5. Slice the French bread into 1¼-inch-thick slices. Place the bread slices on top of the caramel and pecans.

6. Pour the egg mixture over the bread slices. Cover with plastic wrap and refrigerate overnight.

7. In the morning, preheat the oven to 350°F. Remove the French toast from the refrigerator 20 minutes before baking and turn the bread slices over once.

8. Bake the French toast for 35 to 40 minutes, or until the bread has browned lightly on top.

9. When plating the French toast, use a spatula to carefully lift each piece out of the pan and flip it over so that the pecan caramel sauce is on the top. Spoon the extra caramel sauce from the pan over the French toast slices.

10. Garnish with a dollop of crème fraîche, a dusting of confectioners' sugar, and a few raspberries.

Things to Do

Spend a Day at Sea

Captain Tom and the Atlantic Seal Cruises are something of an institution in Freeport, having set sail for the first time some 26 years ago. Would-be sailors can have an adventure-filled day that includes a visit to Eagle Island, formerly owned by Admiral Robert E. Peary, who led the first successful expedition to the North Pole in 1909. Once ashore, tour Peary's summer home and hike the island's trails. Enjoy some beachcombing and catch a glimpse of seals at Casco Bay's seal resting area. Other tours include Seguin Island Lighthouse, seal and osprey watching, and fall foliage tours. Visit www.atlanticsealcruises.com for more information.

THE CAPTAIN LORD MANSION

The innkeepers celebrated the 200th anniversary of the Captain Lord Mansion in 2014. The Mansion, which has been a bed and breakfast since 1978, has earned the reputation of being romantic and luxurious. Inside, a spiral staircase leads up to an octagonal cupola that offers spectacular views. Guests can enjoy some pampering at the onsite day spa or explore other attractions in Kennebunkport, a coastal town that offers sailing, fishing, and kayaking as well as galleries, antique stores, and other shops.

Captain Lord Mansion

6 Pleasant Street
Kennebunkport, ME 04046
207-967-3141
www.captainlord.com

French Breakfast Puffs

Guests at the inn rate these tasty muffins as their favorite breakfast items.

Mansion Stackers

This dish is very simple to prepare—the only element that has to be "made" is the sauce—but it is one of the inn's most requested dishes, proving that food doesn't have to be complicated to be good!

Creamy Cheese Sauce

Try this tasty sauce as a topping for Mansion Stackers.

Mushroom Quiche

This breakfast quiche is rich and flavorful.

French Breakfast Puffs

Yields 12 muffins

⅔ cup soft margarine or shortening

2 large eggs

1½ cups granulated sugar, divided

3 cups all-purpose flour

1 teaspoon salt

Scant ¼ teaspoon nutmeg

3 teaspoons baking powder

1 cup whole milk

½ cup (1 stick) salted butter

1 teaspoon cinnamon

1. Preheat the oven to 350°F. Lightly grease a 12-cup muffin tin.

2. Use a spatula (not an electric mixer) to combine the margarine and the eggs in a medium bowl until well blended. Set aside.

3. In a separate bowl, blend 1 cup of sugar with the flour, salt, nutmeg, and baking powder.

4. Blend the dry ingredients into the wet ingredients until well mixed, alternating with milk by thirds.

5. Spoon the batter into the muffin cups, filling them to the top, and bake for 15 minutes, or until golden brown.

6. While the muffins cool slightly in the tin, melt the butter in a small bowl in the microwave.

7. In another small bowl, mix the remaining sugar with the cinnamon.

8. Remove the warm muffins from the tin, dip the tops in the butter and then in the cinnamon-sugar mixture, and serve immediately.

Mansion Stackers

Yields 4 servings

4 frozen Maine potato pancakes

8 large eggs

1 to 2 tablespoons half-and-half

Pepper

8 medium-thick slices deli ham

Creamy Cheese Sauce (page 231), for garnish

1. Preheat the oven to 350°F.

2. Cook the potato pancakes for 1 hour, or until brown and crisp.

3. Whisk the eggs with half-and-half and season with pepper.

4. Scramble the eggs to desired doneness.

5. Heat the ham in a microwave on medium heat for 2 to 3 minutes.

6. Place 2 potato pancakes on each plate. Put a slice of ham on top of each pancake and top with one-fourth of the scrambled eggs. Spoon cheese sauce over the top and serve.

Creamy Cheese Sauce

Yields about 3 cups

2 tablespoons salted butter

1½ tablespoons cornstarch

¼ teaspoon dry mustard

½ teaspoon salt

2 cups 2% milk

2 cups grated sharp cheddar
cheese

¼ teaspoon cayenne pepper

1. Melt the butter in a saucepan over medium heat. Stir in the cornstarch, dry mustard, and salt and cook, stirring constantly.

2. Add the milk and continue cooking, stirring constantly, until the sauce begins to thicken and bubble.

3. Stir in the cheese and cook until the cheese is melted, about 3 to 5 minutes.

4. Sprinkle in the cayenne pepper and fold it into the sauce.

Mushroom Quiche

Yields 8 servings

1 small onion, chopped

1 cup sliced fresh mushrooms

3 tablespoons salted butter

5 large eggs

1¼ cups half-and-half

1 teaspoon salt

¼ teaspoon dry mustard

2½ cups grated cheddar cheese

1 pie crust for a 9-inch pie plate

Grated nutmeg, for sprinkling
on top

1. Preheat the oven to 350°F.

2. Sauté the onion and mushrooms in butter in a medium frying pan over medium heat until soft and the onions are translucent, about 3 to 4 minutes.

3. Beat the eggs, half-and-half, salt, and dry mustard in a bowl until well mixed.

4. Add the sautéed onions and mushrooms to the egg mixture. Stir until well mixed.

5. Add the cheese. Stir until well coated.

6. Pour the mixture into the pie crust. Sprinkle the top with grated nutmeg and bake for 50 to 60 minutes, or until a knife inserted in the center comes out clean.

FIVE GABLES INN

Guests at the Five Gables Inn, set in a 200-year-old village, can enjoy scenic views of the lobster boats bobbing in Linekin Bay from their rooms or from the inn's porch. Swimming, boating, fishing, and other seaside activities abound. In addition to a sumptuous breakfast, the inn serves a formal tea each afternoon.

107 Murray Hill Road
East Boothbay, ME 04544
207-633-4551
www.fivegablesinn.com

Crab and Sherry Crêpes with Roasted Red Pepper Coulis

You may adjust the amount of sherry in this elegant
breakfast entrée up or down to suit your taste.

Carrot Cake Pancakes

All the delicious flavor of this beloved cake is found in these pancakes—
now you can really have dessert for breakfast!

Blackberry Bread Pudding

This is a delicious way to enjoy blackberries when they are in season and abundant.

Tasty Tidbit

Another type of pudding known virtually only in New England is Indian pudding.
Made with cornmeal boiled in milk, then thickened with molasses and steamed for
a long time, it is one of the first recipes America could call its own.

Crab and Sherry Crêpes with Roasted Red Pepper Coulis

Yields 8 servings

8 8-inch crêpes, homemade or purchased

2 tablespoons unsalted butter

1 cup canned crabmeat (claw is fine), chopped rough

6 large eggs, beaten

¼ cup 1% milk

3 ounces cream cheese, cut into ½-inch chunks

⅛ cup dry sherry

Salt and freshly ground pepper

2 tablespoons finely chopped fresh parsley, plus more for garnish

Roasted Red Pepper Coulis (page 235), for drizzling

Chopped parsley, for garnish

1. Preheat the oven to 200°F. Place the crêpes in a dish, cover loosely with foil, and put in the oven until ready to fill.

2. Melt the butter in a large frying pan over medium heat.

3. Add the crabmeat and sauté for 2 to 3 minutes.

4. Whisk the eggs and milk together and pour over the crabmeat.

5. As the eggs begin to cook, add the cream cheese and sherry and scramble. Season with salt and pepper and add the parsley. Cook over medium-to-low heat until the eggs are mostly done. (They will continue to cook even after the heat is turned off.)

6. Spread a small scoop of the egg mixture across each warm crêpe and roll up.

7. Place the crêpes on a serving platter, drizzle with coulis, and garnish with parsley.

Roasted Red Pepper Coulis

Instead of roasting one of the red bell peppers, you may substitute roasted pepper from a jar, but the flavor is not quite the same. The coulis can be made a day ahead. Store, covered, in the refrigerator and reheat when ready to use.

Yields about 1 cup

2 red bell peppers, divided

¼ cup chopped shallots

2 garlic cloves, chopped

2 tablespoons olive oil

¾ cup chicken stock

1 tablespoon balsamic vinegar

Salt and freshly ground black pepper

1. Preheat the oven to 400°F (375°F if using a convection oven).

2. Place 1 red bell pepper on a small low-sided sheet pan lined with parchment paper and roast in the oven for 15 to 20 minutes. Turn the pepper over and continue roasting until soft and blackened, at least another 40 minutes.

3. While the first bell pepper is roasting, chop the remaining pepper.

4. When the roasted pepper is blackened, put it on a cutting board and cover with a mixing bowl to trap the steam for about 15 minutes. This will allow the skin to slide off easily.

5. In a large saucepan over medium heat, sauté the shallots, garlic, and chopped raw pepper in olive oil until the pepper has softened and the shallots are translucent but not browned, about 3 to 5 minutes. Add the chicken stock and simmer until the sauce has thickened, about 15 minutes.

6. Slide the skin off the roasted pepper, remove the seeds, and roughly chop.

7. Transfer to a food processor, along with the sautéed pepper and shallots, and purée. Add the balsamic vinegar and season with salt and pepper. Serve warm.

Carrot Cake Pancakes

Yields 6 to 8 servings

1 cup all-purpose flour

1 teaspoon baking powder

½ teaspoon baking soda

½ teaspoon salt

½ teaspoon cinnamon

¼ teaspoon nutmeg

⅛ teaspoon ginger

1 large egg, lightly beaten

1 cup buttermilk

2 tablespoons light brown sugar

1 teaspoon vanilla extract

2 cups finely grated carrots

Cinnamon Syrup (below)

Cream Cheese Drizzle
 (page 237)

1. In a small bowl, mix together the flour, baking powder, baking soda, salt, cinnamon, nutmeg, and ginger. Set aside.

2. Whisk the egg and buttermilk together in a medium bowl, then mix in the brown sugar and vanilla.

3. Stir the carrots into the egg mixture.

4. Pour the egg and carrot mixture over the flour mixture and fold gently to combine.

5. Heat a frying pan or griddle and grease with unsalted butter. Pour ¼ cup of batter for each pancake onto the prepared pan. Cook for 2 to 3 minutes, or until bubbles form on top. Flip and cook for another 2 to 3 minutes, or until golden. Add more butter as necessary between batches.

6. Arrange the pancakes on a platter. Spoon on some syrup, top with a little cheese drizzle, and serve.

Cinnamon Syrup

Yields about 1 cup

1 cup pure maple syrup

2 tablespoons unsalted butter

½ teaspoon cinnamon

1. Combine all the ingredients in a small saucepan.

2. Bring to a boil, reduce the heat, and simmer for 2 minutes.

Cream Cheese Drizzle

Yields about ½ cup

4 ounces cream cheese, at room temperature

¼ cup confectioners' sugar

2½ tablespoons 1% milk

½ teaspoon vanilla extract

2 pinches cinnamon

1. Combine all the ingredients in a small saucepan.
2. Bring to a boil, reduce the heat, and simmer for 2 minutes.

Blackberry Bread Pudding

Yields 8 to 12 servings

8 large eggs, lightly beaten

1 cup heavy cream

4 cups half-and-half

2½ cups granulated sugar

1 tablespoon vanilla extract

1 teaspoon cinnamon

½ teaspoon nutmeg

¼ teaspoon salt

1 loaf (16 ounces) Italian bread

2 cups fresh blackberries, rinsed and drained

Confectioners' sugar, for garnish

1. Preheat the oven to 350°F. Grease a 13 x 9-inch oval baking dish.
2. In a large bowl, mix together the eggs, heavy cream, half-and-half, sugar, vanilla, cinnamon, nutmeg, and salt.
3. Cut the bread, including the crusts, into 1-inch cubes. Place enough in the prepared baking dish to mostly cover the bottom.
4. Sprinkle about one-third of the blackberries over the bread cubes. Use half the remaining bread for another layer and top with another third of the blackberries. Layer in the rest of the bread and finish with the remaining blackberries. (The layers will not completely cover each other and will blend together.)
5. Pour the egg mixture evenly over the bread and blackberries. Cover and let sit for 1 hour prior to baking. You can also cover and refrigerate overnight if you wish, but in the morning, let it sit out for 2 hours before baking.
6. Bake uncovered for 1 hour and 20 minutes, or until golden brown.
7. Let the pudding sit for 20 minutes before serving.
8. Dust the top of the pudding with confectioners' sugar, cut into squares, and serve.

THE KINGSLEIGH INN

Situated on Mount Desert Island, home of Acadia National Park, the Kingsleigh Inn boasts guestrooms with stunning water views and private decks from which to enjoy them. A fine example of Queen Anne Victorian architecture, this turn-of-the-century inn has steeply pitched roofs and a cedar-shingle and pebbledash exterior with sea stones hand-embedded in the stucco.

373 Main Street
Southwest Harbor, ME 04679
207-244-5302
www.kingsleighinn.com

House Specialties

Individual Blueberry Soufflés

You can easily double or triple this recipe to make as many servings as desired.

Lobstah Eggs

A Down-East treat that's rich and delicious.

Blueberry Gingerbread

Traditional gingerbread gets a flavor twist with the addition of sweet blueberries.

Tasty Tidbit

Lobster, now considered a luxury, used to be known as the "poor man's protein." When European settlers first came to North America, lobsters were so plentiful that they supposedly washed ashore in piles up to two feet high!

Individual Blueberry Soufflés

Yields 2 servings

3 extra-large eggs

½ cup half-and-half
or whole milk

1 teaspoon granulated
sugar

5 slices raisin bread,
cubed

½ cup wild Maine
blueberries

2 ounces cream
cheese, cubed and
divided

Confectioners' sugar,
for garnish

Maine maple
syrup or 1 recipe
Blueberry Sauce
(below), for serving

1. Preheat the oven to 350°F. Coat 2 8-ounce ramekins with vegetable cooking spray.

2. Whisk the eggs, half-and-half, and sugar in a medium bowl.

3. Stir in the bread cubes and let soak for 15 minutes, tossing occasionally to help the bread absorb the egg mixture.

4. Divide one-third of the bread cubes between the two ramekins. Sprinkle half of the blueberries and half of the cream cheese over each layer of bread. Divide another third of the bread cubes between the ramekins, then sprinkle the remaining blueberries and cream cheese over the second layer of bread. Top the ramekins with the remaining one-third of the bread cubes. Pour any remaining egg mixture over the last layer of bread in each ramekin.

5. Bake for 35 minutes on a baking sheet, or until puffed and browned and a knife inserted in the center comes out clean. If the soufflés are browning too quickly, drape them with foil.

6. Let the soufflés rest for 15 minutes, then run a knife around the edge of each ramekin, unmold the soufflé, and place it right side up on a serving plate. Dust with confectioners' sugar and serve with Maine maple syrup or blueberry sauce.

Blueberry Sauce

½ cup wild Maine blueberries

¼ teaspoon cornstarch

1 tablespoon granulated sugar
(optional)

1 teaspoon freshly squeezed
lemon or orange juice

1. Combine 1 tablespoon of water with the blueberries, cornstarch, and sugar, if using, in a small saucepan and bring to a boil.

2. Boil for 1 to 2 minutes, stirring occasionally, until the blueberries begin to burst.

3. Remove the saucepan from the heat and stir in the fresh juice.

Lobstah Eggs

Yields 8 to 12 servings

18 extra-large eggs, lightly scrambled

1 cup sour cream

½ cup sundried tomatoes in oil, finely chopped

3 to 4 lobsters (1¼ to 1½ pounds each), steamed, shelled, and coarsely chopped

10 ounces fontina cheese, coarsely grated

⅓ to ½ cup fresh basil leaves, julienned with scissors

1. Preheat the oven to 350°F. Coat a 13 x 9-inch glass baking dish with vegetable cooking spray.

2. Place the scrambled eggs in the baking dish and "chop" with a spatula to create an even base. Add dollops of sour cream, let sit for a few minutes, and then spread to evenly cover the eggs.

3. Sprinkle the sundried tomatoes, lobster, cheese, and, finally, the basil leaves over the eggs.

4. Cover the dish with foil and bake for 30 minutes, then uncover and bake until the cheese has melted, about 10 minutes more. Cover and let rest for 10 to 15 minutes. Cut into squares and serve.

Blueberry Gingerbread

Yields 3 mini loaves

1 cup blueberries, fresh or frozen

½ cup canola oil

1 cup granulated sugar

3 tablespoons molasses

1 extra-large egg

2 cups all-purpose flour

½ teaspoon ginger

½ teaspoon salt

½ teaspoon nutmeg

1 teaspoon baking soda

1 teaspoon cinnamon

1 cup buttermilk

1 cup walnuts, chopped (optional)

1. Preheat the oven to 350°F. Coat 3 mini loaf pans (approximately 8 x 4 x 2½ inches each) with vegetable cooking spray.

2. Rinse and dry the blueberries on paper towels.

3. Whisk together the oil, sugar, and molasses in a large bowl. Whisk in the egg.

4. In a smaller bowl, combine the flour, ginger, salt, nutmeg, baking soda, and cinnamon.

5. Add the dry mixture to the oil mixture in thirds, alternating with the buttermilk and ending with the dry mixture. Beat well after each addition.

6. Gently fold in the blueberries and walnuts, if using.

7. Divide the batter into the prepared pans. Bake for 30 to 35 minutes, or until a toothpick inserted in the center comes out clean. If the loaves are browning too quickly, cover with foil. Cool on a rack.

NOBLE HOUSE INN

The Noble House Inn was built in 1903 as the home of Winburn M. Staples, a local politician, prosperous businessman, and state senator. In the mid-1940s, Dr. Fred Gilbert Noble purchased the house for his family. The inn retains many of the relics from its previous lives. Among them is a grand piano, manufactured circa 1898 by the Gildemeester-Kroeger Company of New York. The company was formed when Henry C. Kroeger, Steinway's piano foreman, decided to break away from his employer and go out on his own. Maine's Lakes and Mountains Region, where the inn is located, offers many opportunities to explore and enjoy the great outdoors.

81 Highland Road
Bridgton, ME 04009
207-637-3733
www.noblehousebb.com

Wild Maine Blueberry French Toast with Blueberry Syrup

This is a great dish for company because all the work is done the night before. At the inn, this French toast is served with a side dish of carrots and dried cranberries.

When wild blueberries are in season, pick and freeze them to make this dish during the winter. Freezing wild blueberries takes a bit of patience, but the reward is delicious, flavor-bursting fruit all winter long. Gently wash the blueberries and lay them out on paper towels. Cover them with another layer of paper towels and let dry. Freeze the blueberries in a single layer on a cookie sheet. When frozen, put the berries in freezer bags or containers.

Wild Maine Blueberry French Toast with Blueberry Syrup

Yields 8 to 12 servings

Note advance prep time.

12 slices Texas toast or thick-sliced Italian bread, cut into 1-inch cubes

2 packages (8 ounces each) cream cheese

2 cups wild Maine blueberries, fresh or frozen

12 large eggs

1 cup 2% milk

1 cup half-and-half

1 teaspoon vanilla extract

⅓ cup Maine maple syrup

Blueberry Syrup (page 245), for drizzling

Confectioners' sugar, for garnish

1. Grease or spray a 13 x 9-inch baking dish.

2. Cover the bottom of the baking dish with half the bread cubes.

3. Top the layer of bread cubes with cream cheese. (Cut the cream cheese into small cubes or pinch off small amounts as you work so that there will be cream cheese in each bite.)

4. Sprinkle the blueberries over the cream cheese.

5. Use the remaining bread cubes to cover the blueberries.

6. In a large bowl, mix the eggs, milk, half-and-half, vanilla, and maple syrup, or put it all in a blender and pulse to mix.

7. Pour the egg mixture into the baking dish, making sure to cover the entire top layer of bread with some of the liquid.

8. Cover the dish with foil coated with vegetable cooking spray and refrigerate overnight.

9. In the morning, remove the baking dish from the refrigerator and allow it to sit out for 30 to 45 minutes before baking.

10. Preheat the oven to 350°F.

11. Bake covered for 30 minutes, then remove the foil and continue baking for 30 to 40 minutes more, or until the top has browned.

12. Remove the French toast from the oven and let it rest for about 20 minutes before cutting.

13. Drizzle the syrup over the French toast, dust with confectioners' sugar, and serve.

Blueberry Syrup

Yields 1 to 1½ cups

1 cup granulated sugar	1. Mix the sugar and 1 cup of water in a medium saucepan and bring almost to a boil.
2 tablespoons cornstarch	2. Mix the cornstarch in a small cup or bowl with just enough water to make a slurry with no lumps. Pour this into the sugar water mixture, stirring to mix.
1 to 2 cups wild Maine blueberries	3. Cook just at a simmer or low boil, stirring regularly, for 3 to 5 minutes, or until the liquid thickens to the consistency of syrup.
	4. Add the blueberries and simmer for another 10 minutes or so.
	5. Sauce can be covered and refrigerated for up to 3 days or frozen for 6 weeks.

Things to Do

Take a Boat Ride

Hundreds of lakes and ponds dot the Maine Lakes and Mountains Region, and there are a multitude of ways to get out on the water. Here are a few to consider:

The Songo River Queen II (www.songoriverqueen.net)
Take a ride on Long Lake aboard this replica of a Mississippi River paddleboat. Day and sunset cruises carry riders past beautiful mountains and impressive lakefront properties.

Sebago Sailing (www.sebagosailing.com)
This is the only company that offers sailboat rentals in the Maine Lakes area. Lessons, charters, and cruises are also available.

Mast Cove Seaplane Base (www.mastcoveseaplane.com)
This excursion provides spectacular views of the lakes and mountains from both the water and the air.

THE OXFORD HOUSE INN

The Oxford House Inn was designed by renowned architect John Calvin Stevens and is an outstanding example of Mission-style architecture. The circa 1913 house was erected on part of the foundation of the Oxford Hotel, a 100-room resort that burned to the ground in 1906. The Foxes, a family of lumber barons, spared no expense on their home, and the inn's local tight-grain oak floors, imported Cyprus woodwork, and leaded-glass built-in cabinets are all original.

548 Main Street (Rt. 302)
Fryeburg, ME 04037
207-935-3442
www.oxfordhouseinn.com

Sour Cream Coffee Cake

A sweet way to start the day is with a slice of this fruit-filled coffee cake.

Smoked Bacon, Kale, Roasted Tomato, and Chèvre Frittata

This is a great recipe in the summer when kale and tomatoes are plentiful.

Sweet Additions

Although blueberries are used here, the Sour Cream Coffee Cake recipe lends itself very well to using other seasonal or even dried fruits. Cherries, peaches, strawberries, pineapple, or cranberries are all delicious in this coffee cake.

Sour Cream Coffee Cake

Yields 16 slices

Batter:

¾ cup (1½ sticks) unsalted
   butter, at room temperature.

2 cups granulated sugar

2 large eggs

½ teaspoon vanilla extract

2 cups all-purpose flour

2 teaspoons baking powder

¼ teaspoon salt

1 cup sour cream

1 cup fresh Maine
   wild blueberries

Topping:

¼ cup (½ stick) unsalted butter

½ cup all-purpose flour

¼ cup raw sugar

½ teaspoon cinnamon

1. Preheat the oven to 350°F. Lightly grease a 13 x 9-inch cake pan, then line it with parchment paper and grease again. (This will make it easy to remove the whole cake at one time to cut into pieces. If you plan to cut and serve from the pan, just grease the pan.)

2. Cream the butter and sugar until light and fluffy.

3. Add the eggs one at a time, mixing after each egg, until incorporated. Mix in the vanilla.

4. Mix the flour, baking powder, and salt together in a medium bowl. Add to the batter in fourths, alternating with sour cream, until just combined.

5. Fold in the blueberries.

6. Spoon the batter into the prepared pan.

7. Put all the topping ingredients in the bowl of a food processor with a metal blade. Process until the consistency of coarse sand.

8. Sprinkle the topping evenly over the cake batter.

9. Bake for about 45 minutes, or until a cake tester comes out clean.

Smoked Bacon, Kale, Roasted Tomato, and Chèvre Frittata

Yields 4 servings

6 slices applewood-smoked bacon, cut into ¼-inch pieces

1 tablespoon extra-virgin olive oil

1 cup kale, torn into small pieces

½ cup roasted tomatoes, homemade or purchased

7 large eggs, beaten

2 ounces chèvre

1. Preheat the broiler on low with the rack in the middle position.

2. Render the bacon in an 8-inch nonstick, ovenproof pan on medium heat. Drain off the fat once cooked, about 4 minutes.

3. Add the olive oil and kale to the bacon and sauté 2 to 3 minutes until the kale is wilted.

4. Add the roasted tomatoes and toss a few seconds, just to heat.

5. Add the eggs and scramble until very soft set, about 2 to 3 minutes.

6. Add the chèvre a teaspoon at a time and very gently mix in so there are still chunks.

7. Place the pan in the oven and finish cooking until the eggs are just set, about 5 to 10 minutes. Remove from the oven and let sit 2 to 3 minutes to firm up.

8. Remove the frittata from the pan, cut into wedges, and serve.

INDEX

ACKNOWLEDGMENTS

There are several people I would like to thank for helping make this book come to pass. First, Nancy Hall of The Book Shop, Ltd., who liked the idea enough to take it to publishers, and who offered me the opportunity to write the book. Her inquisitive mind, quick and resourceful problem-solving skills, and genuine kindness and compassion make her one of the best people I have ever worked for.

Anyone who has done a book before knows it takes a team, and this one would never have come together without the incredibly creative design skills of Tim Palin and the meticulous copyediting of Linda Falken—thank you both.

I am grateful for the assistance of Renee Flowers, Director of Marketing for Select Registry (www.selectregistry.com), a hospitality organization of premier inns, bed and breakfasts, and small hotels throughout North America, for putting me in touch with a number of exceptional bed and breakfasts and inns for this book.

Most of all, thank you to my husband, Paul, who is always very supportive of my work as well as a great travel partner, and to my children Melissa, Paul, Melanie, and Madeline, who pick up the slack at home to make writing possible. Last, but most definitely not least, thank you to the rest of my family, friends, and parish family who, in many ways known and unknown to them, helped me run this race.

PHOTO CREDITS

iStockphoto: pp. 53, 57, 59, 65, 83 (bottom), 103, 107, 119, 133, 139, 151, 161, 170, 189, 203, 218, 227, 247; Thinkstock: pp. 8, 11, 39, 43, 49, 50, 55, 81, 83 (top), 92, 115, 117, 118, 131, 134, 163, 176, 179, 209, 211, 213, 214, 229, patterns throughout; Dreamstime: p. 63; Theresa Kapusta: pp. 14, 15, 16; Bryan Still: p. 26; Catherina Strong: pp. 28, 30; Wendy Carlson: p. 33; Barbara Rylander: pp. 42, 43; Rose Schaller Photo: p. 52; Elizabeth Campbell Photography: pp. 68, 69, 71, 142; Christian Giannelli: pp. 94, 98; Zig Guzikowski: pp. 100, 101; Peter Finger: p. 104; Brian Lavall: p. 105; Jonathan Ralston: pp. 108, 109, 111; Charles Smiler: pp. 112, 113; Lyn Norris-Baker: pp. 140, 143; ClearEyePhoto: p. 146; Jaime Lopez: pp. 147, 148; Jumping Rocks Photography: pp. 172, 173, 174, 182, 186; Deposit Photo: p. 179; Diane Endo: p. 183; Scott Thomas: p. 222; Scott Gile: pp. 223, 225; Brian Cervini: p. 242

PERMISSIONS

p. 13: *The Fox and the Pineapple*, by Brian Keith Stephens, reproduced by permission of the artist; p. 215: quote by Paul Theroux used by permission from *The Atlantic*